SOM
journal
9

HATJE
CANTZ

Contents

Peter MacKeith, Michelle Addington, Peter Rowe, and Stefan Behnisch, outside Maison de Verre, November 16, 2012

On Authority

Peter MacKeith

Introduction

The thematic emphases of *SOM Journal* 9 and its predecessor *SOM Journal* 8 (2012) oscillate between examinations of design teamwork and collaboration, and design leadership and authorship. While these issues have been a constant thread of discussions inside the editorial board over the last two years, more importantly, we perceive their resonant strength in the world of professional practice.

As the introduction to *SOM Journal* 8 concluded: "There is an alternate history of architecture and design to be presented, documented, examined, and critiqued: the architecture and design that emerges out of teamwork, out of design collaboration, and an alternative model of design leadership, relying on multiple streams of information, knowledge, and wisdom. Such a history, such an appreciation, by definition would be not one of individuals, but more of collaborative enterprises, cultures, and societies. It is both a history and an ongoing contemporary narrative, of course, and one that requires many contributions and many advocates, but it is nonetheless an essential comprehension to bring forward into the profession, into architectural education, and into the public mind. Such has been the understated ambition of *SOM Journal* 8 and *SOM Journal* 9." Thus, to the shape and content of *SOM Journal* 9, beginning with the esprit of the design jury review and continuing with an overview of the essays, interviews, and commentaries giving depth to the discussion.

I. 31 Rue Saint-Guillaume, Paris

In November, 2012, the professional jury appointed to review SOM projects for inclusion in *SOM Journal* 9 gathered in an inner courtyard off the Rue Saint-Guillaume in Paris, deliberated for three days at the near-mythical Maison de Verre, the early modernist masterpiece and collaborative production of architect-furniture designer Pierre Chareau, architect Bernard Bijvoet, and craftsman-metalworker Louis Dalbet. Within the Maison's luminescent glass-block walls, and enveloped in the Maison's extraordinary screens, partitions, and furnishings, jury members Michelle Addington, Hines Professor of Sustainable Architectural Design at Yale; Stefan Behnisch, HFAIA, principal partner of Behnisch Architekten; and Peter Rowe, the Raymond Garbe Professor of Architecture and Urban Design at the Harvard GSD, reviewed the submitted SOM projects in the same double-height *salle de séjour* once animated by the conversations and passions of Walter Benjamin, Louis Aragon, Paul Éluard, Jean Cocteau, Yves Tanguy, Joan Miró, and Max Jacob.

Since the Journal's inception, jury proceedings have been organized outside of SOM offices to ensure a clear independence of the review process. But while previous jury locations have been modernist masterworks selected more for their magnetic appeal and inspirational character, the settings for the juries of *SOM Journal* 8 and 9 have had an implicit didactic quality as well—an understated pedagogical ambition relevant to the linked editorial themes of these two editions of the *Journal,* so as to reinforce to the jury, to those who had submitted work for review, and to our readers, the thematic emphases of *SOM* 8 and 9: teamwork/collaboration and leadership/authorship in design.

Faithful readers of the *Journal* will recall that the jury for *SOM* 8 convened in the Abbaye Royaumont, the thirteenth-century French monastery which was the site in 1962 of the first declarative meeting of the CIAM breakaway group of modern architects, urban designers, and design thinkers who, despite their internal differences, came to be known collectively as Team 10. The opportunity to convene the jury for *SOM* 9 in the Maison de Verre was no less intentional—neither fortuitous nor grandiose in thinking, although the timing of the jury meeting relied on the good will and generosity of American collector Robert Rubin, now the devoted owner and restorer of the Maison. Rather, the design and fabrication history of the Maison rendered it absolutely desirable and appropriate as the backdrop to the growing vision for *Journal* 9's editorial contents, so focused on examinations of design leadership and authorship in relation to the contemporary necessities of design teamwork and collaboration.

The conventional understanding of the Maison as a masterwork attributable only to Pierre Chareau, and at that, a masterwork of surpassing and unrepeatable mannerism in conception and execution, is not supported by the facts of the historical record, nor by the experience of the design today. The Maison de Verre is, instead, a demonstration of the precise opposite, of productive dispersed authorship and collaborative design, of mutually respectful and equivalent relations between designers and fabricators, of the fundamental collaborations required by the client, the urban context, and the immediate contingencies of the building site, of the harmony of multiple details and building elements artfully brought together into an elegant ensemble.

"Architecture is a social art," wrote Pierre Chareau in 1937, commenting upon the Maison de Verre, five years after its completion. "The architect can only create," he continued, "if he listens and understands the voices of millions of men, if he suffers as they do, if he struggles along with them, to save them."[1] From this idealist perspective of design and social responsibility, it is only a short step to an equally ideal and conjunctive approach to design itself, as an endeavor both individual and collective, both intellectual and manual, both spatial and material. The architectural historian Brian Brace Taylor, in his assessment of the Maison de Verre, emphasizes Chareau's fervent encouragement of a "team-spirit" among all who worked on the design and fabrication of the Maison, and the collective valuation of Chareau, Bijvoet, and Dalbet as equal partners is clearly evidenced in the authors' plaque adorning the front façade. Brace Taylor is even more emphatic in a historical-critical assessment of Chareau: "He was deeply committed to a quest, embodied in his collaborative approach with Dalbet and others: namely, a quest for quality of conception through the intimate association of innovative craftsmanship and intellectual artistic creativity in the modern age."[2] And were we to take the conventional depiction of Chareau as the lead designer, we would still contend intellectually and practically with his role as defined by his French professional title, given his lack of formal architectural training—that of *ensemblier*. On the surface, the *métier* outlines a balancing of architect, furniture

designer, and decorator, but the role suggests also the responsibility to bring together diverse interests (clients, trades, bureaucrats, financiers) and elements (enclosures, furnishings, details) elegantly and harmoniously, in the common cause of the larger ensemble of the intended design.

In these multiple ways, the siting of the *SOM Journal* 9 jury in the Maison de Verre was more than coincidental in time or place, it is in fact intentional and emblematic. The glass walls of the Maison, together with the stone walls of the Abbaye Royaumont, materially and demonstratively bracket the intellectual spectrum of these two issues.

II. Leadership and Authorship

With the Maison de Verre as an instructive context for the jury review and *Journal* 9, it is a pleasure therefore to include in these pages the re-publication of Kenneth Frampton's seminal essay on the house, which first appeared in the pages of *Perspecta, The Yale Architectural Journal* (No. 12), in 1969. Professor Frampton's contributions to the *SOM Journal* span its history; he has been no less a part of *Perspecta*'s own history over its many years in print. His research and reflections on the Maison de Verre (undertaken together with Robert Vickery and Michael Carapetian) in *Perspecta* 12 marked his entrance into American architectural publications, following his appointment to the faculty of architecture at Princeton in 1965. Regrettably, limitations of page space have prevented us from reprinting in its entirety the essay's extensive accompanying documentation of the house, in meticulous and thorough measured drawings and photographs, but these have now passed into the general literature of the house in the ensuing thirty-five years.

But Professor Frampton's concluding words of his 1969 assessment possess a vitality undimmed by time, and a renewed relevance to the contemporary moment of the *SOM Journal*: "It is curious that, thirty-seven years after its erection, a purpose-made house should still have the capacity to exert a powerful influence upon our imagination. Perhaps, it is because it continues to offer through the fluidity of its plan, the standardization of its components and the mobility of its parts and through its clear assembly of public and private spaces within a single envelope, a general model from which to evolve

solutions to some of the indeterminate problems of our epoch."[3] While the emphasis in the 1969 examination of the house was fixed on its spatial, technical, and material aspects, the provocative "general model" of the Maison de Verre suggests another parallel set of investigations and possible models of design, into the social and economic character of its design and fabrication, and into both its design authorship and collaborative production.

This concept of a "general model" of design leadership is given precise and relevant individual characterization in Nicholas Adams' essay on SOM's Gordon Bunshaft, "What Convinces Is Conviction." Professor Adams continues his ongoing research and reflection on the history of the SOM practice, now measured over several issues of the *Journal*, but here with a concentration upon Bunshaft's iconic, but shifting, leadership presence in the practice over a period of several decades. As Adams details, the conventional perception of this central SOM figure as silent, decisive, and proudly individual—the consummate hero-architect—is far too limited and not nearly as nuanced a portrait as Bunshaft (and SOM) deserves. Indeed, Bunshaft may have once arrogantly joked that the "only reason his name was not on the masthead was that the initials of the firm would have been S.O.B.," but by the twilight of his career, he acknowledged publicly that the success of the practice was due to the ethos and efforts of a much larger group of designers. The progress of his work and leadership in the firm demonstrates a notable adaptability to circumstances, to collaborative design, and to recognition of the work of others. Adams' essay reveals an architect epitomizing essential qualities of "conviction and adaptability, of integrity and excellence," qualities he asserts are of

continuing relevance to the contemporary practice's evolving partnership structure and identity.

In turn, the *Journal's* subsequent interview with John Harwood, professor of architectural history at Oberlin College and author of *The Interface: IBM and the Transformation of Corporate Design*, opens up the more general historical and societal issues of decision-making and agency crystallized by the Bunshaft example. Harwood's work in this area is rapidly taking shape through a number of publications and venues, as his discussion suggests, but his methodological focus, as he says, is to attempt "a description of the corporate situation" of any architectural commission and to view design decisions as "complex … aggregations of human endeavor." Harwood eschews simplistic views of authorship as "insufficient to describe our own world," and while finding contemporary relevance in Henry Russell Hitchcock's important 1947 essay, "The Architecture of Bureaucracy and the Architecture of Genius," also finds Hitchcock's default to the artistic "genius" of Frank Lloyd Wright a rear-guard action. For Harwood, "the corporate nature of architecture production is unavoidable," and moreover, this "corporate situation" is one characterized and conditioned by the continuous advance of technologies—in the contemporary moment, the unavoidable presence of digital technologies (an issue of authorship and agency taken up next by Thomas de Monchaux). Importantly, Harwood concludes our discussion with a reference to SOM's Nathaniel Owings and his later contemplations of the design corporation he had helped found, suggesting that an acceptance of the fundamental changes in the architectural profession will lead to a better imagining of a corporate architectural practice.

Thomas de Monchaux's essay, "Clear All Ghosted," focuses our attention squarely on the contemporary conditions of architecture practice and identifies immediately an entirely destabilized condition of architectural authorship. The condition prevails, de Monchaux proposes, in a postmodern culture of mythical signature architects branding collaborative endeavor, even as poststructuralist analysis of that same culture insists on the "authorless-ness" of any cultural expression. De Monchaux's third destabilizing factor and the essay's ultimate subject is "the presence of computing and the history of mechanical and digital computation in architecture." This is a history too close and too immaterial to be examined with traditional tools of analysis; de Monchaux makes extensive use of his own interview with Greg Lynn, architect and curator of the 2013–14 exhibition *Archeology of the Digital*, as well as associated documents and statements from that exhibition's major protagonists, Peter Eisenman, Frank Gehry, and to a lesser extent, Bernard Tschumi. De Monchaux's rapid-fire and fluent analysis is no less incisive, noting for instance, that the literary-critical and philosophical ambitions of the architects—a dream of "authorless-ness"—were enabled and realized by the potentials of digital design. His essay suggests that these same architects, in their individual searches for "the perfect procedural process," in fact have less knowledge of the character and effect of the digital tools and techniques that now enable their authored/authorless work. De Monchaux's essay is a cautionary reflection on the coincidence of "early digital design" and architectural ambitions in poststructuralist culture; his identification of the digital and philosophical "ghosts" haunting the contemporary moment of design practice is open-ended, but well-observed.[4]

Journal 9's final editorial essay, "Leadership/Teamwork in Practice," is in fact a constructed discussion between principal designer Helle Søholt of Gehl Architects/Urban Quality Consultants and Olafur Eliasson of Studio Olafur Eliasson, focusing on their respective collaborative approaches and inter-disciplinary design practices. The discussion is itself a second exercise in collaboration across the design culture, following on the previous one in *SOM Journal* 8 with Michael Bierut of Pentagram and Sandy Speicher of IDEO, with the ambition to draw upon the wisdom of those engaged in modes of design practice different from that of SOM, either in scale of practice, or in design character all together. The discussion is based on the belief that architecture can learn more for its sustenance from other creative fields, whether the visual arts, the literary arts, or the design arts. Eliasson's emphasis in his large studio practice on his team members' developing a sense of "co-responsibility," and Søholt's equal emphasis on the act of "co-creation" in their urban design works undertaken with city planning offices, municipal authorities, and community stakeholders, are both important interpolations towards a contemporary form of design practice, balancing individual

identities and authorship with the advantages of a collaborative approach. There is much to be gained from their reflections.

As codas to the collected essays, *New Republic* architecture critic Sarah Goldhagen and educator Sarah Whiting, Dean of the Rice University School of Architecture, provide short perspectives and commentaries on the central issues of the *Journal,* each relative to their vantage point on contemporary architecture culture. Goldhagen's continued advocacy for a "situated" comprehension of architecture echoes John Harwood's, perhaps, but she goes further, advocating more vocally for the recognition in critical and historical terms of "the collective paradigm" of architecture's production. This has been an ambition in *Journals* 8 and 9 as well, as stated in our initial introduction. For Whiting, "(A)rchitecture is nothing other than a means of assembling relations across its many constituent threads," and the emphasis in education must be on refining the decision-making skills of designers in the assembly and judgment of those complex relationships.

III. In Transition

So, too, has been the emphasis in the *Journals* 8 and 9 overall, and it is hoped that the essays in these twinned issues will both provoke thought and refine judgment. The projects selected by the *SOM Journal* 9 jury, as well as their edited observations and commentaries, presented here following this introduction, are further evidence of these ambitions.

I began my association with this SOM enterprise through work as a member of the design review jury for *SOM Journal* 7. It has been a privilege to subsequently provide editorial leadership to *SOM Journal* numbers 8 and 9. As with my colleague in architectural education Sarah Whiting, I too have approached the responsibility of the *Journal* from the perspective of the students we work with and the young professionals we encourage, as well as from the vantage point afforded by SOM's worldwide practice. As *SOM Journal* 10 will be prepared under new leadership, I conclude my work in the editorial role both sobered and encouraged. The enormity of the urban, landscape, and building design tasks demonstrated within these SOM surveys reveals the desperate need for more fully prepared architects—prepared to work across the range of design scales—perhaps particularly at the scale of the city and the landscape—prepared to work with greater cultural awareness and greater historical sensibility, indeed prepared to work more cross-culturally and collaboratively, and still on the most intimate, focused, and material of terms. SOM, through these juried reviews of projects, and through this *Journal* of history, theory, and criticism, demonstrates an encouraging commitment to understanding its own trajectory in the contemporary landscape of "more," as well as to contributing positively to the intellectual depth of the discipline.

As before in *Journal* 8, the conception and production of *SOM Journal* 9 has relied on much collaborative enterprise. The attentive and responsible work of jury members Michelle Addington, Stefan Behnisch, and Peter Rowe provided for a sound, thorough review of the SOM project entries. Contributing essayists Kenneth Frampton, Nicholas Adams, Sarah Goldhagen, John Harwood, Thomas de Monchaux, and Sarah Whiting, and design practice respondents Helle Søholt and Olafur Eliasson, must all be recognized for their time, energy, and thought. Amy Gill has been a patient, steadfast managing editor throughout the entire process. Lastly, appreciation and admiration must be given to the architects, designers, consultants, and staff of the SOM offices who participate in the firm-wide collaborative effort, and whose work is represented in small and large ways in these pages.

1. "La Maison de Verre," Le Point (May 1937), as quoted in Brian Brace Taylor, *Pierre Chareau: Designer and Architect* (Cologne, 1992), p. 51.

2. Brace Taylor 1992 (see note 1), p. 27.

3. Kenneth Frampton, "Maison de Verre," in *Perspecta, The Yale Architectural Journal* (12), p. 83.

4. "I was struck, while on a recent jury at a prestigious East Coast architecture school, by the pervasive influence of a new, perhaps more virulent breed of formalism, more virulent because it was posed under the banner of a neo-avant-garde technological determinism. The nexus of this formalism lay in advanced computer modeling techniques generated out of complex algorithms that produced parametric processes of enormous complexity and consistency, replete with their own variability and distortion. The range, variety, and energy of this work should have appealed to me personally, not only because of my memories of that particular institution as a bastion of intellectual conservatism, but also in part because this cutting-edge-process work was close to an idea of autonomy inherent in such authorless processes. Instead, I felt that something was radically wrong, something that speaks to a more general problem of architecture today. It was an autonomy freed from any passionate or firm ideological commitment." Peter Eisenman, commentary given as part of a symposium marking his eightieth birthday at Princeton University School of Architecture. The prestigious school he referred to was the Harvard GSD.

Jury Observations

As outlined in the introduction, the jury assembled for *SOM Journal* 9 enjoyed a quietly didactic setting and the discussions among the jury members were spirited, good-humored, and productive for all concerned. In keeping with common practice, the editor and managing editor served only as facilitators for the jury evaluations, either through organization of the jury schedule or through moderation and encouragement of the jury discussions. The jury proceedings were recorded and fully transcribed, but the publication of the full transcription is not provided here, an approach first adopted in *SOM Journal* 5. Rather, the jury commentary has been transcribed and edited into a series of four project-centered jury discussions.

As a group the jury sounded a number of consistent observations throughout the evaluation process, a set of perceptions and concerns that were stimulated initially by the review of SOM projects and then at a later stage, through reflections on the current state of architecture, urban design, and environmental engineering. The relation between the projects and the larger context of architectural culture and the world economy was very much in the jury's mind throughout the discussions.

OBSERVATIONS ON THE PREMIATED ENTRIES:

Baietan: Heart of Guang-Fo Urban Design Master Plan

Peter MacKeith (PM): *SOM is now engaged with masterplanning commissions worldwide, with a particular emphasis in the last several years in China. The Baietan Master Plan project was distinguished by all members of the jury as being the best of the many master plans submitted for review. Why has it achieved that status?*

Peter Rowe (PR): Of all the plans in China, this was the most interesting and there are several reasons for me. One reason is that the process on the front end of the project was collaborative and productive. The process seems to have started with a collaborative "kick-off," a deployment of the design team's assets to look widely and deeply at the issues. The project involved the full range of clients and necessitated a very serious engagement with that range of stakeholders: the city planning bureau, the land development group, the urban planning studio. This has meant a full court press on the part of Guangzhou to engage with SOM, and SOM has responded accordingly.

The second thing about the project and its process is that from the beginning the design team speaks about "the Lingnan style," and about response to local culture and context; this project has responded very well to these contexts and conditions. It's far more sensitive in its contextual approach than most other projects of its type that we reviewed, despite it being a very big project spread out over a substantial site, including variations in elevation. It's very "Guangzhou," in its grain of spaces and buildings; in nineteenth-century images of the city, that same feeling would be evident. The way in which the project distributes itself over the topography and the green spaces is also in the spirit of the Lingnan style—essentially with the southern part of China and the Guangdong province in particular.

But as importantly, the design produces an image of a contemporary city that is plausible, reasonable, and one I wouldn't mind being in, quite frankly. It's scaled appropriately, and it has a mix of buildings to be expected in a development of this kind.

Michelle Addington (MA): The big positive of the project is one of its primary initial premises: the design's adaptation to future climate change, rising sea levels, and increased cycles of flooding. Drought is not mentioned, but that's probably going to be an issue ... and it might have been a further set of diagrams and design responses. But flooding is going to be a significant factor in this location and the way the design team has thought about multiple arenas for managing climate change, and consequent sea level rise, and flooding is really strong. Design must begin with this as a baseline as opposed to something to be avoided and here that baseline seems to be more accepted—rather than simply as having some kind of sea wall. The project is fine-grained from a point of building distribution, but there's also a graining that deals with how water is being mitigated and managed for a site at multiple scales. All of that is one of the strongest parts of this master plan.

There's one negative aspect here and it doesn't have to do with the scheme: it's simply the presentation documents: the last page indicates a thirty-two percent savings in foregone power plant construction and an eighty percent waste savings. A slew of numbers are given, but there is no causal correlation to anything that shows up in the design representation, so none of these numbers connect to anything specific that is going to happen. The closest that the presentation comes to a credible demonstration of these claims in the design is in the depiction of the shaded street.

Stefan Behnisch (SB): It's a strong scheme. True, the final images and numerical claims of the presentation are more of a charter than a proven set of concepts. But a further strong point is in the treatment of the realities of the brownfield areas of the site. The tendency in China with new development projects has been to just go to the next available site—to leave the older brownfield site as it is and to proceed to ruin the new site. The rest of the proposal I would see as a charter and a set of goals. The project would be fully convincing if, for each of the graphs concluding the presentation, there was a page to show a concept of how that goal would be achieved.

PR: From a planning and urban design point of view, it's the best scheme in this group. I can't speak to the claims made with regard to sustainable development—there's an attempt being made there—but that's not the gist of this anyway. The project is a highly urban scheme in a circumstance where it should be, and comes across as a plan that is really quite workable. And by the way, the project is a breath of fresh air compared to Beijing and other city developments with immense city blocks and the resulting monotony. The design team has broken away from that normal superblock planning scheme that is all too common in China these days—an approach which has all sorts of problems with respect to transport, flexibility, habitability, and so forth. The grain of the design is absolutely correct; it allows them to integrate a considerable amount of existing structures—desirable for historical conservation reasons and utterly appropriate given the site's very strong place in Chinese history. It does so rather effortlessly.

Colpatria Calle 84

SB: This project has much to appreciate. It's a little bit of an exception in this review because there's not much residential design in the submitted group of entries. Architecturally, the project is challenging and the design team has responded well in terms of floor plans, daylighting, etc. The project isn't a tower, but rather a horizontal volume and has, for an urban context, pretty sophisticated floor plans. The possibilities to vary floor plans—bigger apartments, smaller apartments—are notable and suggest a very flexible planning strategy.

To its credit, the building takes the pragmatic approach: pragmatic, but state-of-the-art. The brick construction is pragmatic. Admirably, the design team resisted the temptation to make just another box. The façades deserve more elaboration; the project would be even more successful with differentiated sides. Only the sun-shading strategy seems a little bit flimsy. The section is great, really well done and informative; although even more information on how it really does work would be useful. The section shows that the project has huge potential for two story window gardens.

A last note: when the design team prepares for the next jury review, my advice would be, cut to the chase! If the material doesn't have the appropriate image to represent an idea, then a hand sketch for the benefit of the jurors would be fantastic.

MA: This project presented itself immediately as right for Bogotá; it makes a lot of sense in its climate and light design approaches. Bogotá is an unusual location in that it tends to be cooler and it stays cool pretty much year round. Without knowing too much about the amount of solar radiation or cloud cover there or not, it's still possible to admire the well-reasoned approach being taken to climate and light conditions. The design deals with solar thermal for hot water and for floor heating and doesn't try to shoehorn in a new or more advanced technology. Instead, the design employs systems technologies that are more appropriate and feasible—ones that make sense for a building like this. Normally, the use of thermal mass in many locations can be disconcerting or overreaching, but this is a reasonable place to use a little bit of thermal mass. The cold water going into the floor system as well as hot water is equally thoughtful. The design choices are all actually reasonable—and admirable! It's not the sexy systems, it's the reasonable ones.

All of the interior punctures are very appealing, although the images don't show the windows as being operable. The sections suggest incredible possibilities to do with natural ventilation, but without visible openings on the exterior, it's not clear if those possibilities are being considered. Is that just an oversight or is this really not ventilated?

PR: Bogotá is starting to come alive again! Knowing the Calle 84 pretty well, the use of brick and bent forms is not unusual in that area: it's an area that architects from the modern period in Colombia worked really thoroughly and

the sinuous form is not out of place. The design provides a fantastic view across the savannah, and also rather straightforwardly and interestingly deals with a sloping site. It's at grade level on one side, and the other side has a sort of courtyard.

As a proposition, several further aspects are notable. One is the idea that slightly irregular forms are contextually viable in this area of Bogotá, and in Bogotá in general. The materials are done right: the brick, in particular, is a sound choice—it's already a substantial part of the materiality of residential architecture in Bogotá. But the second aspect is the fact that there's a set of horizontal planes into which can be plugged the idea of the relatively wealthy person's villa. And the project seems to amply accommodate that with a double story maisonette, with ample spaces, commodious planning, and sufficient flexibility. There are only three types in the plans, but the idea of having a platform that an inhabitant can infill with a luxury villa is provocative.

In fact, the sections show that there's a fair amount of variety that can be introduced as far as the units are concerned. The design exploits the conventional notion of stacking units together to make the assembly language of residential units. With this scheme of horizontal slabs, this project presents a vertical car park version: the ability to drive right up to your sky-villa and boom, there it is baby. There might be even more variations on the system, but it's still good.

New Los Angeles Federal Courthouse

PM: *You've been interested throughout our review in sections and floor plans, and day-lighting. This project has a sloping site, it's a box that has to fix itself to a sloping site … surely we can talk here in a most focused way about site strategy, plan strategy, section strategy, and day-lighting strategy.*

SB: This is a very good government building, when lately the idea of a good government building has become something of an oxymoron. The building's scale is appropriate to the urban site and it works well in the urban setting. It's a sophisticated building for Los Angeles. I like the outcome. I like the way it's very boxy, but in LA everybody thinks they have to be so expressive now, everybody goes wacky—this doesn't and succeeds all the more. At the same time, as a government building, it doesn't look like a fortress. It creates a plinth without getting carried away, and has a side building for some service functions and offices. The atrium works well.

The design employs a good day-lighting strategy. What is the reduction in incident solar reduction by the façade? The problem is that the sun-shading is inside, which is always, once the heat is inside, very hard to get out again. The section shows movable panels as the solution to that condition. There are some huge dropped ceilings, the kind of dropped ceiling that has to be sprinklered—probably also a special condition because of the large rooms. But all in all, a very good building.

MA: The GSA's expectations and requirements for new courthouse design are challenging. Here, the design team was really stuck with the depth of the floor plate; there's not much that can be done with it, but the design response is strong. And too, in this day and age in terms of a government building's defensible borders—particularly trucks and access to trucks—the only alternative is to build a giant barricade. The box makes the most defensible building. Again, this is all very tough with such a deep floor plate and here, the design response has been strong.

The general day-lighting approach is strong as well. I appreciate the fact that the light courts are actually very narrow and really well placed in the building. One image needs further attention: the courtroom day-lighting strategy … I am not sure there is ever such a sun angle in Los Angeles. The closest angle might be noon on a summer solstice which in Los Angeles might hit a peak of seventy-five degrees. Much of the design is about day-lighting but there should be more demonstrations of the strategy. The

undulating façade and the screening system are good extensions of the day-lighting and thermal control strategy.

PR: This project just looks like a courthouse, like a good, well-thought through government building. The front of the building is very well done, ascending two floors before the overhang. The middle part where the light is allowed to come in is very well done, too; the courtyard is nicely landscaped. Altogether, in the city and as a building, very well done.

The Strand, American Conservatory Theater (A.C.T.)

PR: This is an attractive design, in fact it's beautiful—can we just say that? I think the approach here is one of SOM's strengths: work that may not be out on the edge, but rather work that is extremely well done—to the point of being beautiful. This small theater is an example of that, in the nature of the commission, in the intimacy of its scale. The way the components have been assembled together is compact and wonderfully worked out. There is an experiential set of spaces that are exceptional, especially the front part.

The new design has worked within an existing shell, moving the gallery out which didn't exist in the original. The balanced riser system on the steps works well. A lot of intelligent work has been accomplished here, in a rather condensed commission. It doesn't miss too many tricks. A projection screen is a very good idea too. Are the wind-driven rooftop ventilators a good idea? I imagine they are.

MA: It's well done. What I really appreciate, as most theaters use displacement ventilation, is the fact that this displacement ventilation system can be tied into an actual ventilation system and go ahead and use it that way since it's already set up to do that mechanically. Wind-driven rooftop ventilation works in such theaters. The design thinking in all of this is intelligent: it takes advantage of San Francisco's mild climate.

There's been a proliferation in recent years of the

dedicated concert hall, or opera house, or chamber music venue. This is a black box theater: there's no fly tower, and it needs a greater purposefulness for all uses. It's got to be economical to run and it's got to be economical for the client to support. While that's not the architectural issue for SOM particularly—it's an essential issue of the client in this particular location which is totally high-end. So while the theater is not totally high-end, the design result is beautiful functionality.

I love the divergence from the standard black box theater … what so many people have done to make a black box theater more functional is to eliminate fixed seating. What the SOM design team has done here is actually add that functionality into the lobby by using a scrim layer for film projection. A separation is needed between the black box and the lobby, but what is normally a functional wall providing separation now provides continuity between the two spaces. Dual functionality without having to be all-purpose: it's a new way of thinking about the space and use of the theater, providing a means to have specialization without being hyper-specialized, without trying to be an all-purpose, flexible space. This is the next generation of design thinking—by taking advantage of different characteristics and surfaces, more than one kind of audience is possible. All of this beautiful functionality and all about as low cost as possible—which is all the more remarkable.

SB: The design is calm, understated, and thorough. That's the old 1953 façade? That is also cool with everything else on Hollywood Boulevard. The lobby is good, the section is good: this is a good, small theater, well done.

LARGER ISSUES

Following the specific review of SOM projects and a subsequent selection of a number of those for recognition, the *SOM* 9 jury expanded their discussions based on more general issues raised by the project review. As can be seen in their edited observations below, these issues ranged from digital design tools to design process to design research.

PM: *At the conclusion of the project reviews, the discussion had already begun to situate these SOM works in a larger context relative to other SOM projects, to other buildings and to larger issues. Could we turn to this perspective now: to understand this current body of work and where it might be situated in a larger spectrum? Peter Rowe commented early on about the idea of community becoming fetishized, Michelle Addington had talked about the prevalence of badly done wind studies, and Stefan Behnisch focused more on day-lighting as a design issue. These are all issues that go beyond the work itself and lead to more general discussion.*

ON DIGITAL DESIGN TOOLS

MA: I think our discussions on the use of simplistic wind and day-lighting studies come from the same concern. There's been a proliferation of "dumbed-down" tools built for architects who are trying to visualize these environmental factors. But there's a critical difference between something being visualized and something representing simulated behaviors. But because these tools are now available, you see a proliferation of wind studies in architectural presentations (which at one time would have only been done by engineers)—and even more so with day-lighting studies.

SB: This ties in to our observations in the project reviews. Environmentally responsive design has become so specialized and complex and architects have to rely on these parameters so much: it's not the amateur hour anymore in calculation or representation. With any good wind study of a master plan, even a practice such as Transsolar can't undertake the calculations anymore because their computers go down—they have to buy time at IBM or the military. There's a reason why this is so complex; the process can't be dumbed down to provide (such seemingly) reliable parameters.

MA: Wind is a much simpler phenomenon than natural convection: it's difficult enough to do the wind study but even tougher to look at density driven convection. Designers using thermal chimneys are already acting on very naïve ideas about how such a chimney performs. When a simplified representational tool is then used to reinforce a naïve belief about how such technologies operate, then problems arise. A designer may not know enough to question the capabilities of that tool … and relies on it too much.

SB: As with structural conceptions, it's possible to work with a rule of thumb to initiate an idea, but beyond that, what is needed is verification and detail—and that's highly complicated. These computational fluid diagrams are a highly complex thing. If architects really do their job and think about space, form, material, and so forth - and bring all the parameters together—to be honest, architects are busy enough with those synthetic concerns to leave the complex calculations to the engineers. These complexities are not something that can be done on the side.

MA: Beyond the complexities of these factors and these tools, there's another concern: that wind as well as day-lighting can be seen as deterministic design factors. Many design proposals suggest that a wind study of a highrise will lead directly to affecting the twist of the façade or the prevalence of openings in the façade. In the project reviews, we saw a number of high-rise designs that looked as if their forms were trying to respond to the wind: it's just bizarre to think about it! There's a false assumption that wind factors like this will lead to an associated formal determination. Most of the day-lighting studies regrettably lead to that kind of formal determinism—where do the louvers go, how do these elements work—all of them were about creating some type of formal response. Far less emphasis or awareness is

demonstrated about actually understanding how the light penetrates through the façade into the architectural space—and much more interest is given to how to articulate the façade. The rational process of the study now overwhelmingly determines the façade: there is an energy reason for it, and then a whole series of justifications for this type of determinism as opposed to some kind of personal (… or even arbitrary …) sensibility.

PR: Strangely, I can find analogous situations in planning and the landscape realm, where extraordinarily provocative swirling diagrams of processes or flows are presented and the resulting parks end up looking exactly like the diagram. With this level of modeling, if the modeling is being employed to find some truth, then a lot of the failures should be displayed as well—an incremental idea of how the best solution was achieved should be given. How do I know these things are optimal? I don't. A plethora of red and green things swirling around in a diagram: it looks great but it's not a proven concept by any stretch of the imagination in terms of the way modelers think of these things. The process of what doesn't really work is vital to the chosen outcome as well. Why a certain conclusion is reached whether optimal or not is another thing entirely: the design decision is made because it's the best. What constitutes best? Its parametricized outcome. Quite apart from the fact that you have dumb models, i.e., the parameterization of this or that design factor is pretty weak in relationship to the physical phenomena that prevails in the world.

There's any number of information modeling programs that are easy to use, and give flashy results and supportive diagrams. But we don't build diagrams—that's not architecture. A diagram is information. In the simulations seen here, it's not clear if that's the best result that one could've obtained with these techniques, nor is it clear that the techniques are even the best available. This is why the Baietan project receives such praise in our evaluation: there is a certain normalcy to it.

SB: These simulations, and modeling in general, are attempts at a more integrated design process. But the essential question is why are the simulations, analysis, and diagramming almost always so self-generated? Wouldn't it be more objective to involve an outside agency? By such a disengagement from the analysis, a design practice would be less tempted to influence the outcome. Such third parties would also have access to better software. Why put your own thumb on the program in your office? You're bound to be wrong, or at least biased in the outcome. As we discussed before, it is good to begin with a "rule of thumb idea," but the best verification and the real advice in these complex cities should come through a third party—one that's not a plug-in, not an in-house SketchUp diagram.

ON COLLABORATION, CONSULTANCY AND DESIGN PROCESS:

PR: This returns our discussion here to another issue raised in the project reviews: the essential need in any project to have the right consultants, the right participants in the design process, and to work with those people at critical junctures in the entire process. There are certain points along the way in the design process where you need to haul these people in, and make sure you've got the right ones. It's not ganging them all up in the front, or ganging them all up in the back, it's somewhere in between. You need to have the sensibility to do that. You need to organize your team so that somebody is sensitive to that set of outcomes.

MA: Certainly there has been a sea change in the field of mechanical engineering consulting, where for many years the tasks were very quotidian, essentially specifying basic types of HVAC systems in buildings. That has dramatically changed: Transsolar, for one, led the charge in bringing the profession forward from being essentially a "trade" and dealing with it as a trade, to now actually

having scientists analyze phenomenon behavior. Regrettably, this change of identity and expertise hasn't yet proliferated nearly as much as it could into the industry. Most of the mechanical engineers currently employed as consultants to architects are more comfortable with the "trade" of engineering than they are at undertaking sophisticated analysis. But, as projects and expectations become more complex, that normative team of consultants is less and less valuable.

Another set of concerns is the "dumbed-down programs" we just discussed. Part of this entire lineage developed from an academic interest in writing advisory software to help architects design more effectively; the idea was that an advisory system would make you more aware of different factors and lead to more optimal design responses. Some of this in fact emerged out of early Doctor of Design theses undertaken at the GSD. Ecotek, for instance, was originally advisory software, one never meant to be a planning tool or simulation tool. But these simulation software programs all come from this lineage of "the architect advisory," intended to keep architects aware early on of these factors and to have that awareness then integrated throughout the design process. There was good intent in this: re-working or enhancing the old classic model of "conceptual design phase-design development phase-construction drawing phase." The advisory software's analysis was to have been integrated into that process so that architects could understand how big the building should be or what is the optimal solar orientation, and so forth. But these "advisors" have gone from being a design assistance tool (and they are no better conceived of than as an advisory tool), to a presumptive modeling tool—to determining the design itself. This condition now hits at the master plan level, and indeed at all different levels and scales of design consideration.

PR: In my design research laboratory we never use the generic off the rack programs, other than big broad platforms like GIS—but even within that we tweak every single thing and we script it. Otherwise, the precision specific to each project is just not there. A normative tool that aims at a general direction will be nearly useless when the specific project has its own conditions and directions.

PM: *Throughout the projects review, there was a consistent reference to discussion of habitability, to the specifics of occupation. Could it be said that there are no parameters for that, that there's no advisory software for that?*

SB: For that we have a brain.

PR: There is a danger in becoming too reliant on the technologies of analysis and assessment, and then going on automatic pilot in design. The questions need to be asked: how are people going to live here? Or work here? Under the sway of this digital/software "technological imperative," very little in the way of narrative of a way of life is expressed (and I'm using the term in a very broad sense), or of how that lived experience actually happens. We should not be making one-dimensional assumptions about living patterns; we should recognize that there are different cultural norms and expectations, ones that design can incorporate and enhance.

ON DESIGN CONCEPTS and DESIGNING FOR DIVERSITY, DEPTH AND CONNECTION

SB: The SOM projects begin with strong, very clear concepts to explain the building's design. Yet, after schematics the designs appear to lose that conceptual strength and become more and more normal buildings. The original intentions appear to have been lost. This is a common occurrence: a great concept sketch—of a layered design, for instance—which then disappears in the subsequent plan formation. As design instructors as much as architects, we tell our students to make that one line sketch, write that one page concept statement and then read it all the way through the design process again and again and again. The strength of the originating concept must be consistently shown in a project.

PR: To approach this subject from another vantage point, beyond the emphasis on an originating concept: the need for diversity and flexibility in plan typologies. Around 1990, especially in residential environments, not only has there been a massive increase in populations to be adequately housed, but also an immense diversification of those populations—and residential design has to respond. Routinely now the best housing projects are designed with up to twenty to thirty plan variations, moving away from the old modernist canon in which five seems to be the limit (except in the Unite d'Habitation). In these diverse circumstances, a generic plan will not be sufficient; the plans provided must be *the right kind* and of sufficient diversity themselves.
On the other hand, at the urban scale of design, SOM's Baietan project has a kind of positive, refreshing normalcy—a quality that promotes a desirable flexibility of spatial inhabitation. My point here is that along with diversity of individual housing plans, flexibility at the urban scale is also needed. And at the urban design scale, SOM does very, very well in the plans that they produce: their work always possesses a good common sense and proposes even inspired solutions to an urban problem.

MA: However, all along the way, I discern another troubling general tendency—and it is one that is as apparent in the work presented in design schools as well. The designs we see all too often exhibit a lack of connection to those who might inhabit one of these apartments, or to the people residing in the houses in the agricultural village. My concern is the disappearance of "the body as subject" in design—that everything now becomes object-centric in design, and that there's a definite distance from that designed object. If the design proposal is a building, for example, the design becomes only about the façade, the exterior surfaces. In our project review here, we saw very little development in any of these interior spaces. We saw more effort on the surface of the object, of the object as a sort of an entire entity, and this approach is as apparent at the urban scale as it is at the individual building scale.

PR: We're dealing with a generation of designers where visceral reactions to the idea of life are few and far between.

MA: Such a disconnect between the process of design and those visceral reactions creates a greater comfort level with the designed object as artifact, rather than as a space, or place, or people, with whom there is a shared connection. There is a generational difference here, I understand. On the one hand we are products of a generation and participants in a generation that believes very strongly in "concept" as a necessary element in design thinking. I don't see that belief in any of our young faculty or our students. At the same time, we also didn't grow up with these rendering tools in order to have a concept be described and represented in many different ways. What we see are a set of rendering tools that make it easier to be object-centric rather than concept driven. The object skins very quickly with Rhino, for instance, and similar software. This is not a discussion of "the death of drawing," but rather in more essential terms of how we come to grips with the loss of concept and the prevalence of the singular object as a form. In these circumstances, with these current tools, it becomes much easier to work the surface of a form than it does to work the section of a form—and with that surface emphasis, of course, our desires for spatial character, for tectonics and for interior atmosphere lose relevance. Whether this is the way things are and will be, and whether therefore we've got to rethink the way we approach design and what we expect from design, is a very real question. Or, do these current circumstances demand yet another change in the practice of architecture?

PM: *It seems there are two things at play here: 1) that modeling software is intended to be advisory but has in fact become deterministic and 2) that representational software is intended to evoke qualitative atmosphere but has in fact led to generic interiors. So what are the escape mechanisms?*

PR: One of the problems with this overly determined precision vis-à-vis the idea is that it stunts the way you think through to true precision. It has the appearance of that and then you get kind of lazy and don't work hard enough. I think you need to have that to really work through some of the issues in an integrated and formal way.

SB: Regarding this question of concepts: do we lose them, do we need them, is it a different generation? Sometimes I get suspicious when I start complaining about today, but still think actually the lack of concept, it's a little bit like social life, we need an idea, we need a concept, and we need the rough sketch to go through. I don't believe in the genius sketch, don't get me wrong, but we need from the rough to the more detailed and refined design. To have a starting point you need a concept. And interestingly all of these pages that we looked at twice all have a concept. The question is how far do they carry them. Was it only a starting point and became a pancaked extrusion? All the ones we carried further resonated in a way because we understood what had been done and were interested. Look at the theater, at the Colombia residential house we interpreted more to it than actually is there. There was an idea in the beginning that got lost but we were able to build it ourselves, but we needed this villa concept and then we said wouldn't it be nice if it were more animated. The LA courthouse, we know there is a lighting issue, which brings us back to the idea that science is not the time for amateur hour. But the concept is clear, it's a courtyard, or two inner-courtyards, it's day-lit, it's a nice space, the circulation areas, it's very clear, it's a good box. And actually LA deserves a good box, so it's fine!

If you think about the ones we could carry further were always those where we understood the concept or even gave the benefit of the doubt in the concept and the ones we lost were the ones where we couldn't find the concept in the second page. I think that's important. The Raffles school is a typical example. We were actually excited about that project in the beginning. So from then we thought how is the concept related to this building? How does it function? Why no trees? Why do you clear the rainforest to put this kind of thing? And why did they add to the concept three-story buildings that have this odd angle in the back? Suddenly the concept was lost for us.

ON DESIGN RESEARCH

PM: *In the last several years, there have been SOM projects that were built, but relied on or referred to applied research from CASE. It would be useful to understand CASE's efforts and their real value as research.*

MA: I admire the work that CASE is doing and I would like to discuss the issue of research in architecture. In the projects we reviewed, there were two that were trying to be research. SOM's relationship with CASE is important for the practice and for us all. We have so few models for applying research to architecture and we all champion this one but what I've always found interesting about this is that it has a tendency to take the much loved object of architecture, the surface, and focuses research on this, making the surface performative, but it comes from not really having a question but more of fulfilling a desire. That's not what research is entirely about. So there ends up being beautiful surfaces, but the decision for them is never been grounded in anything more than, "we want to make a performative wall." That's what is missing from these other two projects is that they're defining themselves as research but there's no hypothesis.

SOM Journal 9
Submissions

100 Mount Street
Sydney, New South Wales,
Australia

AEC-APPS: Architecture,
Engineering, Construction app
database

Beijing Greenland Center
Beijing, China

Beijing Bohai Innovation City
Beijing, China

Grand Hyatt Jeddah
Jeddah, Kingdom of Saudi Arabia

Kuwait University Campus
Gateway
Shadadiya, Kuwait

Lakeside
Chicago, Illinois

Liansheng Financial Center
Taiyuan, Shanxi Province

Nozul Lusail Marina
Doha, Qatar

Panama Government District
Panama City, Panama

Parkmerced Vision Plan
San Francisco, California

Park Riyadh Hyatt
Riyadh, Saudi Arabia

SoBe Park
South Beach, Florida

Son Tra Peninsula
Da Nang, Vietnam

Ssiger International Plaza
Cixi City, Zhejiang, China

The Diagonal Tower
Seoul, South Korea

Cold Bending Glass

Denver Union Station
Denver, Colorado

Gangxia P1 Office Tower
Shenzhen, China

Grand Central Terminal:
The Next 100 Years
New York, New York

LJZ Capital Plaza
Shanghai, China

Nanhu Country Village
Nanhu District, Jiaxing, Zhejiang

Nanjing Xiaguan Riverfront
Master Plan
Nanjing, China

Next C: A Blue City
Tianjin-Binhai Region, China

Platinum Tower
Kuala Lumpur

PS 62: Net Zero Energy School
Staten Island, New York

Raffles American School
Iskandar, Malaysia

Shared Architecture-Structural
Parametric Modeling Research

Wujiang Lakefront Project
Wujiang, China

Baietan: Heart of Guang-Fo Urban Design Master Plan

Guanghzou, China

Designed 2009–10

Baietan occupies the low-lying alluvial plains of the Pearl River Delta in Central Guangzhou. The area is subject to annual flooding from high water in the Pearl River at flood stage, and internal flooding during large rainfall events caused by insufficient detention and drainage capacity. The Pearl River is tidally influenced; therefore any sea level rise amplifies the impact of flooding. The majority of land located in the Pearl River Delta is situated below the projected sea level rise of 1.4 m.

In April 2009, SOM began to work in partnership with local government and other partners in what became an informal, open, and very collaborative design process. A critical first step in the development of the Baietan Master Plan was a weeklong workshop held in Guangzhou. The workshop brought together some eighty people representing a broad cross section of technical and policy experts.

A series of sustainability-integrated planning and design strategies was established during the workshop and guided the overall plan framework. A fundamental aspect of the project's approach was the use of "Transit-Oriented Development" (TOD), which concentrated on over thirty million square meters of high-density, mixed-use development within walking distance of existing and planned transit. Mobility throughout Baietan was enhanced by reorienting the existing road system towards the Pearl River waterfront. Roads were redesigned to provide a clear system of access and wayfinding, while the use of smaller-than-typical blocks enhanced pedestrian movement around the new neighborhoods.

Given the imminent risk of flooding and impact of projected sea level rise, the Baietan Plan proposes a suite of comprehensive strategies that include raising land for key redevelopment areas, establishing stepped wetland levees, and providing an interconnected network of canals and floodable green spaces.

The Guangzhou Steel Plant, Guangzhou Shipyard, Guangzhou Paper Mill, and other large industrial developments, dominate land use in Baietan along with the hundreds of smaller "mom and pop" style industrial operations. Until the last decade all of these sites were generally unregulated by state and local government; it was common for hazardous and regulated chemicals to be discharged directly into waterways and indirectly into the soil and/or groundwater at these sites. The Pearl River is recognized as one of the most polluted rivers in the world, and according to research by World Wildlife Fund, over ninety-two species of freshwater fish found in the river's ecosystem face extinction. In order to transform the river into a habitat capable of supporting local wildlife, a bio-remediation program was created for over 300 hectares of brownfield land. Central Park will be the signature open space of Baietan. Positioned on the former steel mill and shipyard, the diverse botanical programs of this grand public park will act as a "phyto" pump to remove contaminants from polluted soil and groundwater.

Given its strategic location for international trade, Guangzhou has always been a magnet for foreign business. A cross-fertilization of knowledge and technology has created a culture of openness, diversity, and willingness to embrace new ideas, leading to the development of eclectic architectural character, building and spatial forms, and building technologies. There has also long been a sustainable architectural design response to the subtropical monsoon climate and physical features of the natural environment.

The Baietan plan is guided by the intrinsic qualities of Lingnan culture—a reference to the creative influences that distinguish southeastern China from the more formal culture of China's north. Specific Lingnan design strategies presented by the plan include low-rise and human-scaled buildings that reinforce connections to historic structures, canals, landscape corridors, and arcaded streets that provide continuous shade and shelter for the residents and workers of Baietan.

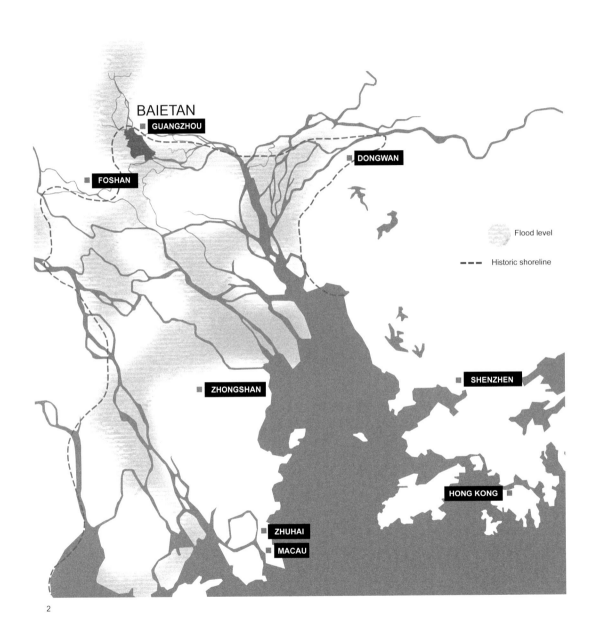

BAIETAN

■ GUANGZHOU

■ DONGWAN

■ FOSHAN

Flood level

– – – Historic shoreline

■ ZHONGSHAN

■ SHENZHEN

■ HONG KONG

■ ZHUHAI

■ MACAU

2

< 1   Aerial view of Baietan area
  2   Project site showing potential sea level rise
  3   Open space system diagrams

Raised land for redevelopment area
Spoils from excavating underground parking garages will be used to raise the land to a minimum elevation of 8.3 meters, which is above the projected sea level rise influenced 200-year flood stage.

Interconnected network of canals and stepped wetland levees
All raised land will drain directly into canals and rivers through an expanded network of canals so the hydrologic burden on the remaining low-lying areas is greatly reduced. Levees will protect existing low-lying land.

Resuscitated riparian corridors
Along the existing waterways of the Huadi River and larger waterways that flow across the Baietan, gentle wetland habitat terraces are established to allow for these lands to naturally refurbish with regional trees, water-loving plants, and wildlife while maintaining the flood control functions.

3

4

4   Baietan physical model looking north
5   Subway transit plan
6   Transit oriented development concept. Compact nodes
     of high intensity, mixed-use developments are located
     within five-minute walking distances of existing and
     planned transit facilities.

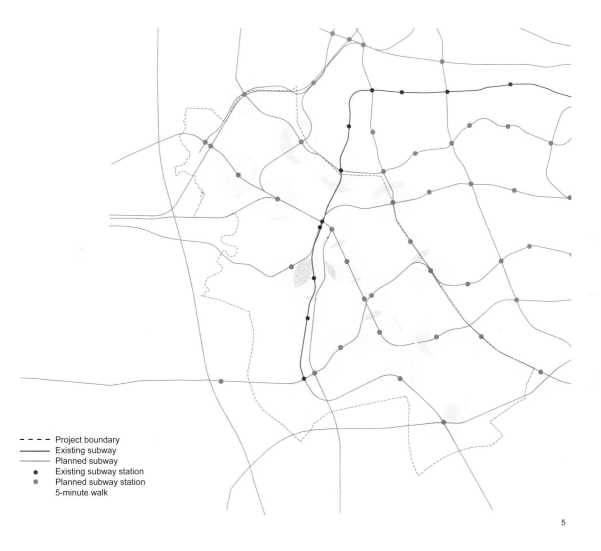

Project boundary
Existing subway
Planned subway
Existing subway station
Planned subway station
5-minute walk

5

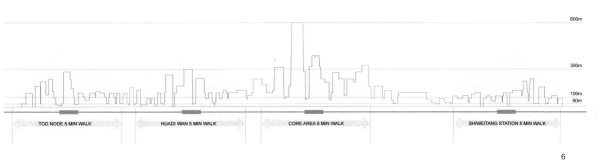

| TOD NODE 5 MIN WALK | HUADI WAN 5 MIN WALK | CORE AREA 5 MIN WALK | SHIWEITANG STATION 5 MIN WALK |

600m

300m

100m
60m

6

A SOY SAUCE FACTORY
B DIESEL ENGINE FACTORY
C GUANGZHOU PAPER MILL
D GUANGZHOU SHIPYARD
E GUANGZHOU STEEL PLANT

7

- - - - - Project boundary
█ Brownfield land
█ Remediated land

8

7   Over 300 hectares of brownfield land, including heavily polluted sites such as the Guangzhou Iron and Steel Mill, Guangzhou Shipyard, Guangzhou Paper Mill, and Guangzhou Diesel Engine Factory, will be remediated.
8   Situated on the former steel mill and shipyard, the diverse botanical programs of Baietan Central Park will act as a "phyto" pump to remove contaminants from polluted soil and groundwater.
9   Rendering of Central Park

9

10 Rendering of proposed Baietan master plan

Colpatria Calle 84

Bogotá, Colombia

Designed 2012–ongoing

Colpatria Calle 84 is a distinguished residential development planned for the northeast section of the La Cabrera neighborhood in Bogotá, Colombia. This capital city sits on a 2700-meter-high picturesque plateau west of the Andes, and enjoys a relatively cool year-round climate. Set in a bustling area, the twelve-story building's design responds with views of the mountains to one side and the city on the other. These enviable surroundings are exploited at three primary scales: neighborhood, building, and unit.

The neighborhood features residential buildings of a variety of scales ranging from two stories to twelve. Unique to the Colpatria Calle 84 site is a ten-meter change in elevation from east to west that creates a private vehicular entrance and service access from Carrera 7A. A private garden, like those found in traditional Colombian homes, is arranged around the perimeter of the site. This helps to keep the site secure and buffer the courtyard from the commuter traffic of Carrera. Carrera 7A, a quieter street on the western side of the site provides a gracious, landscaped, formal entrance to the site.

The primary building façade material of this neighborhood and throughout Bogotá, is a locally manufactured brick. With a nod to this traditional material, Colpatria Calle 84 also uses a locally made precast, beige brick but in a way that injects some nuance into the typical building façade found nearby. Slender fins made from the brick run vertically along all sides of the building, and are arranged in a rhythm that varies in response to the program and at fluctuated angles for prime views and optimal daylight filtering. The scale and placement of the openings in the façade, particularly along Carrera 7, are intended to provide continuity to the urban street wall. The articulated massing of the building creates shading as well as openings for double-height garden spaces for individual units.

At the building scale, an orientation with the long elevations on the east and west maximizes the best exposures for all units. To the east the site is warmed by the rising sun in the morning; to the west it benefits from the sun at the end of the day. The building uses the brick massing to capture the heat of the sun by day and retain it through the evening hours to ensure comfort without the need for mechanical heating systems. Operable windows on both elevations allow natural cross ventilation for cooling during the warmest part of the day.

The building contains about 18,000 square feet of boutique hotel-like amenities on the ground floor. Access is private and it's possible for residents to use the facilities, including a pool, fitness center, and public gardens without ever crossing paths with their immediate neighbors. Four levels of underground parking sit below.

Each unit has been envisioned as a "villa in the sky," with a through-block plan for exposure to all views and cross-ventilation. Generous garden terraces give the units a strong interior visual focus and can be used for dining or relaxation. The individual garden courtyards are arranged vertically and are either double-height shaded spaces or open to the sky. The vertical brick fins continue along these garden perimeters providing a daylight filter along with open views. The interior space planning creates social gathering areas that focus on a traditional hearth, and secluded zones for service functions. Each villa owner will begin the day with vistas of the mountains and end with the drama of city lights.

3

CARRERA 7A

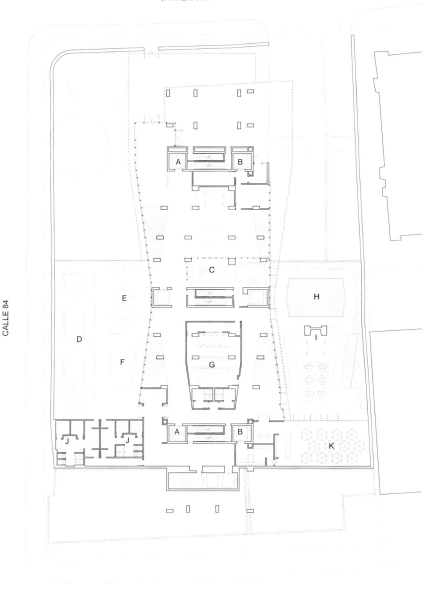

CALLE 84

CARRERA 7

4

A	PASSENGER ELEVATOR	G	SCREENING & PERFORMANCE
B	SERVICE ELEVATOR	H	CHILDREN'S PLAY AREA
C	LOUNGE / LIBRARY	I	FIRE PIT
D	LAP POOL	J	RESTROOMS
E	JACUZZI	K	PRIVATE DINING
F	CHILDREN'S POOL		

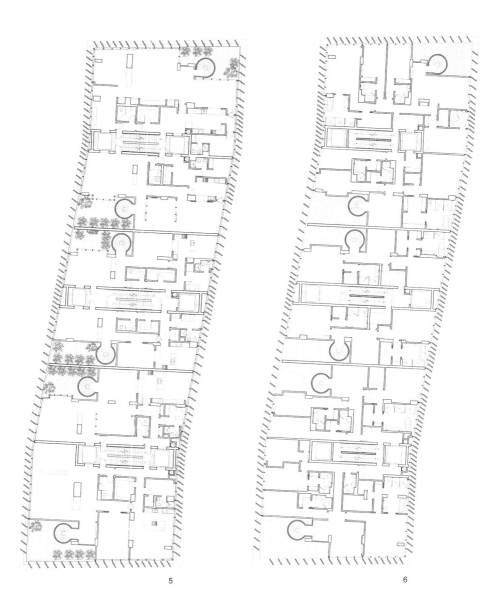

5

6

4   Lower ground floor plan
5   Duplex plan lower
6   Duplex plan upper

7 Building sections
8 Mechanical diagram

7

A   EVACUATED TUBE
    SOLAR COLLECTORS
B   GREEN ROOF
C   DOMESTIC HOT
    WATER RISER
D   HOT/COLD WATER
    RISERS FOR RADIANT
    FLOOR SYSTEM
E   HOT WATER RISER
    FROM SOLAR PANEL
F   COLD WATER RISER
    TO SOLAR PANEL

G   GRAYWATER TO MBR
H   IN-FLOOR RADIANT
    SYSTEM
I   HEAT EXCHANGER
J   SWIMMING POOL
K   DOMESTIC WATER FROM
    MUNICIPALITY
L   HOT WATER RISER FOR
    SWIMMING POOL
M   BOILER
N   DUAL COIL STORAGE TANK

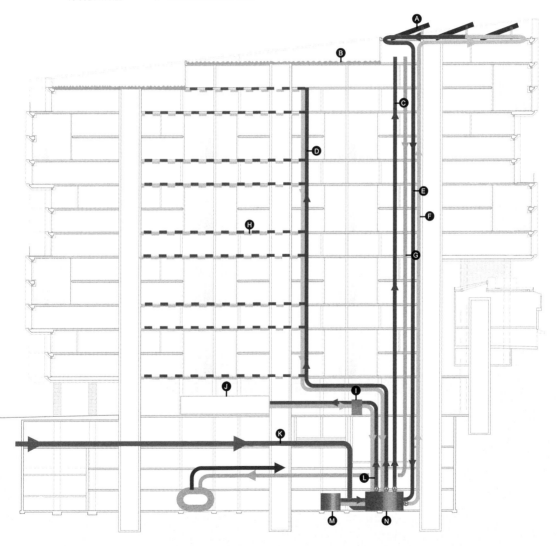

8

9

9 Exterior wall section perspective
10 Exterior wall close-up
11 Detail exterior wall section
12 Detail exterior wall plan
13 View along Carrera 7 >

10

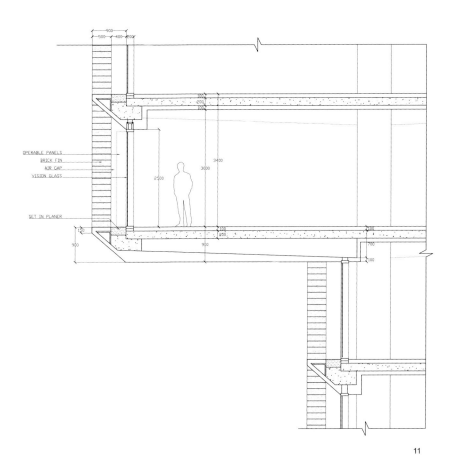

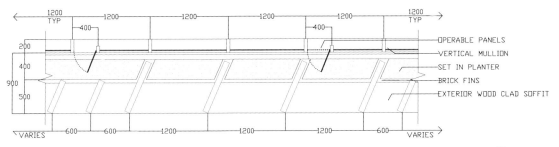

OPERABLE PANELS
BRICK FIN
AIR GAP
VISION GLASS

SET IN PLANER

11

1200 TYP
1200
1200
1200
1200
1200 TYP

400
400

200
400
900
500

OPERABLE PANELS
VERTICAL MULLION
SET IN PLANTER
BRICK FINS
EXTERIOR WOOD CLAD SOFFIT

VARIES
600
600
1200
1200
1200
600
VARIES

12

New Los Angeles Federal Courthouse

Los Angeles, California

Designed 2012–13

The site for the new Los Angeles Federal Courthouse is on the cusp of the Los Angeles Civic Center and the adjacent high-rise Commercial Office District. The site is an important public transportation hub linking downtown Los Angeles and the suburbs. The Metro Rail Civic Center station is across Hill Street, and a future Regional Connector Rail station is planned for one block east.

The design for the new Los Angeles Federal Courthouse represents the rational convergence of the project influences: site, civic character, program, high sustainable performance, and light. With a strong civic presence, the building uses classic design principles such as processional steps, elevated entries with great public spaces, and enduring materials. It is contemporary in form and material, yet reflects the principles of archetypal Federal architecture with a modern interpretation of classic tripartite design: base, body, and cornice.

The program requires a four-courtrooms-per-floor configuration. This, accompanied by the other requisite program functions, including the insertion of a central light court to bring daylight into the public core of the building, lent itself to a square in plan. Additionally, the massing generated by the square plan combined with the number of floors required created a vertical height equal to the square plan's horizontal dimension, resulting in the building's cubic form.

The desire to "float" the cube above the plaza provides an opportunity to create a unique structural concept which sets four robust, hardened concrete cores forty feet back from the corners of the building. These extend vertically to support a two-way steel roof truss system. The roof trusses extend to the exterior building face, allowing the outer forty feet of the cube to hang in tension from the trusses above. This allows the removal of plaza level perimeter columns while providing additional blast stand-off distance for the ground level structure.

The hardscape and planting design is contemporary in form and materials while embracing the principles of minimal, yet accessible public space. The seamlessly integrated landscape is comprised of five areas: streetscape, entry plaza, stepped gardens, interior courtyard, and roof desert gardens.

The stepped gardens are a prominent feature of the concept design and allow the existing site topography to slide underneath the cube, creating juxtaposition between the platonic form above and the existing site topography. These gardens allow for organizational paths of travel to traverse the slopes from Hill Street to the Main Plaza to Broadway, creating places to circulate, congregate, and contemplate away from the building entrance. Species of native California perennial shrubs found within the chaparral ecology form continual bands throughout the gardens, accentuating variations in planted form, texture, and color.

With the surrounding street grid rotated thirty-eight degrees from true north/south, the exterior façade is designed with faceted vision panels rotated to a north/south orientation and thermally opaque panels rotated to an east/west orientation. This provides a forty-seven percent reduction in annual solar radiation and reduces the central plant load by nine percent. The glass façade has a dynamic visual depth due to its faceted assembly, and accentuates the play of light across the façade.

Ensuring the connection between occupant and exterior environment is a driving factor in the design of the interior spaces with almost every space having access to natural light. Highly controlled in-pouring daylight is provided to the courts through high transoms above the judicial bench and from the light court behind the gallery. In addition, floor to ceiling glass is provided in the judge's chambers to provide abundant natural illumination.

The LEED Platinum design incorporates many energy saving strategies including a rooftop photovoltaic array and cohesive water recapture system. Site drainage along with HVAC condensate recovery provides one-hundred percent of the irrigation needs. The project will meet the General Service Administration's 2020 energy target of 35K BTU/GSF annually.

2

3

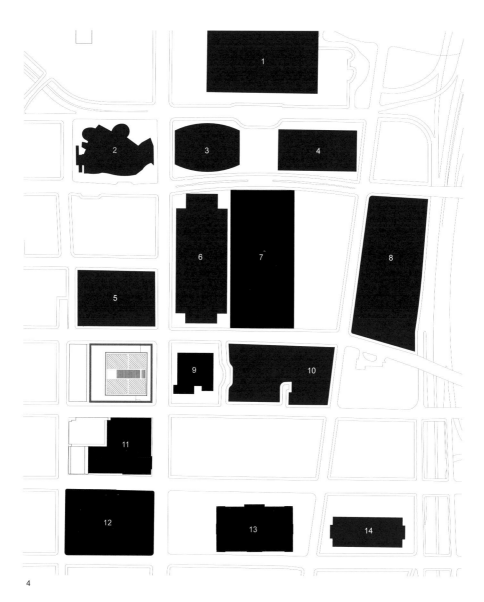

4

1 DEPARTMENT OF WATER AND POWER	8 CATHEDRAL OF OUR LADY OF THE ANGELS
2 WALT DISNEY CONCERT HALL	9 LAW LIBRARY
3 DOROTHY CHANDLER PAVILION	10 LOS ANGELES DISTRICT ATTORNEY
4 LOS ANGELES MUSIC CENTER	11 LOS ANGELES TIMES BUILDING
5 FUTURE GRAND AVENUE PROJECT	12 LOS ANGELES POLICE DEPARTMENT
6 CITY HALL	13 LOS ANGELES CITY HALL
7 GRAND PARK	14 US DISTRICT COURT

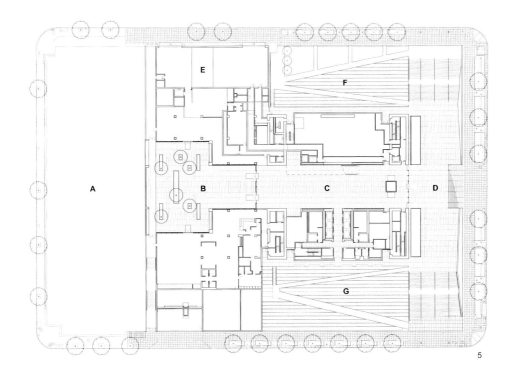

A FUTURE OFFICE BUILDING SITE
B GARDEN PLAZA
C LIGHT COURT LOBBY
D CIVIC PLAZA ENTRANCE
E SALLYPORT
F HILL STREET GARDEN
G BROADWAY GARDEN

6 Typical court floor plan
7 Longitudinal section

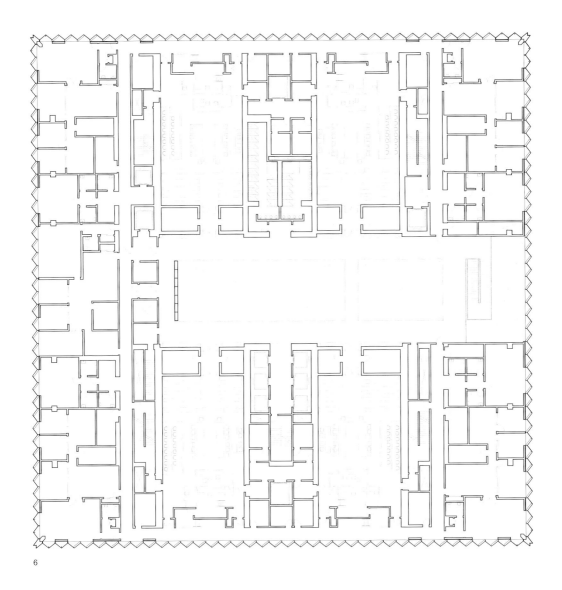

6

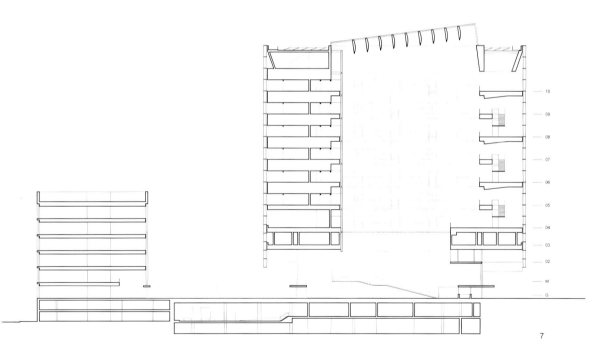

10

09

08

07

06

05

04

03

02

M

G

7

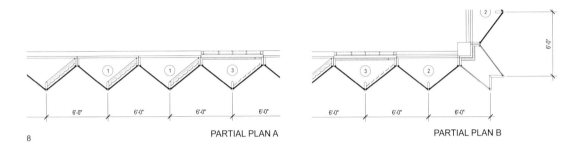

PARTIAL PLAN A

PARTIAL PLAN B

8

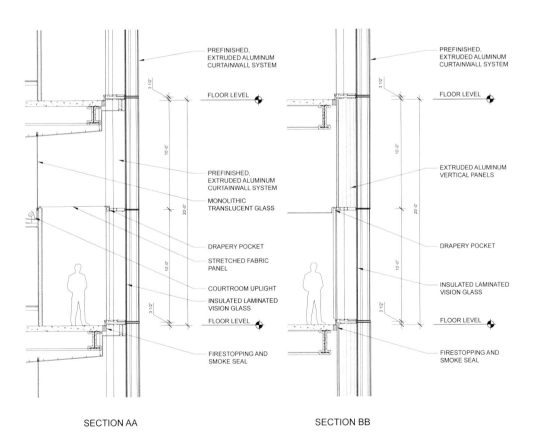

PREFINISHED,
EXTRUDED ALUMINUM
CURTAINWALL SYSTEM

FLOOR LEVEL

PREFINISHED,
EXTRUDED ALUMINUM
CURTAINWALL SYSTEM

MONOLITHIC
TRANSLUCENT GLASS

DRAPERY POCKET

STRETCHED FABRIC
PANEL

COURTROOM UPLIGHT

INSULATED LAMINATED
VISION GLASS

FLOOR LEVEL

FIRESTOPPING AND
SMOKE SEAL

PREFINISHED,
EXTRUDED ALUMINUM
CURTAINWALL SYSTEM

FLOOR LEVEL

EXTRUDED ALUMINUM
VERTICAL PANELS

DRAPERY POCKET

INSULATED LAMINATED
VISION GLASS

FLOOR LEVEL

FIRESTOPPING AND
SMOKE SEAL

SECTION AA

SECTION BB

9

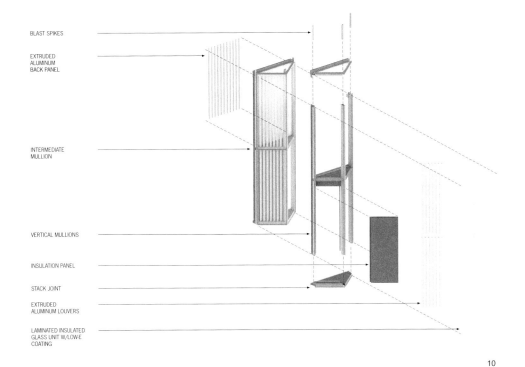

BLAST SPIKES

EXTRUDED
ALUMINUM
BACK PANEL

INTERMEDIATE
MULLION

VERTICAL MULLIONS

INSULATION PANEL

STACK JOINT

EXTRUDED
ALUMINUM LOUVERS

LAMINATED INSULATED
GLASS UNIT W/LOW-E
COATING

10

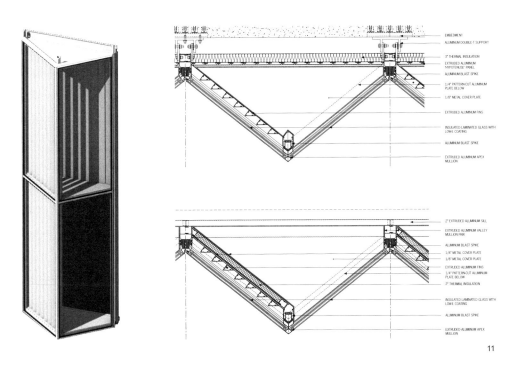

EMBEDMENT
ALUMINUM DOUBLE-T SUPPORT
3" THERMAL INSULATION
EXTRUDED ALUMINUM
'HYPOTENUSE' PANEL
ALUMINUM BLAST SPIKE
1/4" PATTERN-CUT ALUMINUM
PLATE BELOW
1/8" METAL COVER PLATE
EXTRUDED ALUMINUM FINS
INSULATED LAMINATED GLASS WITH
LOW-E COATING
ALUMINUM BLAST SPIKE
EXTRUDED ALUMINUM APEX
MULLION

2" EXTRUDED ALUMINUM SILL
EXTRUDED ALUMINUM VALLEY
MULLION PAIR
ALUMINUM BLAST SPIKE
1/8" METAL COVER PLATE
1/8" METAL COVER PLATE
EXTRUDED ALUMINUM FINS
1/4" PATTERN-CUT ALUMINUM
PLATE BELOW
2" THERMAL INSULATION

INSULATED LAMINATED GLASS WITH
LOW-E COATING
ALUMINUM BLAST SPIKE
EXTRUDED ALUMINUM APEX
MULLION

11

12 Lightcourt lobby rendering
13 Buildiing front rendering

12

The Strand, American Conservatory Theater (A.C.T.)

San Francisco, California

Designed 2012–14

The renovation of the Strand Theater resurrects the derelict hundred-year old movie house on San Francisco's Market Street to provide a highly visible experimental performance space for the city's preeminent theater company, American Conservatory Theater (A.C.T.). The redefined space, which incorporates educational facilities for A.C.T., houses a new 300-seat theater, a 120-seat black box theater and rehearsal space, stage support, public lobby, and cafe. The program is inserted into the shell of the former 800-seat cinema, overlaying essential modern theater elements on top of the raw backdrop of the original building. The design creates inspiring civic theater out of the act of theatergoing by dramatically opening the lobby and façade to the street and sidewalk, energizing both the building and the surrounding neighborhood, representing a key component to the regeneration of this once vital part of the city. The Strand Theater is located between the city's booming retail district and the Civic Center, in the midst of the fast growing tech and residential developments that have recently begun to relocate to the blighted Mid-Market section of Market Street. The neighborhood has witnessed decades of decline and stalled attempts to return to its mid-twentieth-century glory, and the Strand is a key catalyst for the renewal and regeneration of this once great cultural neighborhood.

The centerpiece of the lobby is a full-height fritted glass projection scrim. Lit from above with skylights or with theater lights at night, the scrim creates a modern-day proscenium, framing the movement and social interactions within the open-plan lobby. Along with the café and box office, the stairs and balconies, the scrim acts as a scenic stage backdrop for pre-function gatherings. A central stair is organized around the scrim and links the large theater on the lower levels to the smaller one upstairs, creating a multi-level environment that the audience moves through like a stage set. Like the old Strand's movie screen, the scrim can show projected images that extend the theater experience into the lobby and establish and embellish the production's mood and message.

The scrim also serves as a marquee, providing a supergraphic information display for upcoming shows and events. Even when the theater is closed, the imagery on the scrim transforms the character of the building, projecting the energy of the theater into the street, and to the neighborhood beyond.

A state-of-the-art collection of wind-driven rooftop ventilators draws cool outside air into the large theater volumes and pulls warm internal exhaust air back out, allowing the building to utilize natural ventilation throughout the year. During infrequent warmer periods in the summer and fall months, a supplementary mechanical ventilation system helps offset audience and theatrical-lighting heat loads. Overall building energy consumption is reduced by over thirty percent, as a result.

To be successful, a contemporary urban theater must respond to a broad range of artistic attitudes and attract a broad audience demographic. To do so, the Strand design team has invented a newly engineered flexible seating riser to accommodate quick and efficient reconfiguration of the theater seats. The flexible seating serves and inspires wide ranging artistic visions—modern, dynamic, young, traditional, formal, and informal—while shaping a new model for drama and theater. As Carey Perloff, the Artistic Director of A.C.T. stated, "The design is porous, energetic, witty, and welcoming, allowing the Strand to become a lively destination for a wide variety of cultural experiences and spontaneous gatherings. I hope the imaginative conception of the interior spaces will inspire artists to create visionary new work in a supple and flexible environment. The Strand will belong to the whole community, a beautiful series of spaces where we can come together and tell our stories."

2

3

4

1	HERBST THEATER	11	GOLDEN GATE THEATER
2	SAN FRANCISCO OPERA	12	THE WARFIELD
3	DAVIES SYMPHONY HALL	13	CRESCENT HEIGHTS
4	CITY HALL	14	TWITTER BUILDING
5	ALIOTO PLAZA	15	AVALON BAY COMMUNITIES
6	BILL GRAHAM AUDITORIUM	16	TRINITY PLACE
7	ASIAN ART MUSEUM	17	FEDERAL BUILDING
8	ORPHEUM	18	CITY PLACE
9	THE ART INSTITUTE OF CALIFORNIA	19	MINT PLAZA
10	UN PLAZA		

JOIN US FOR A ONE-NIGHT ONLY READING OF THE LANDMARK
MARRIAGE EQUALITY PLAY "8"

ENDGAME *AND* PLAY   SEP 13 - OCT 7 2012 WINNER OF THE 2011 TONY AWARD F

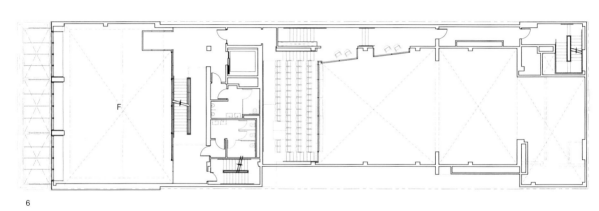

6

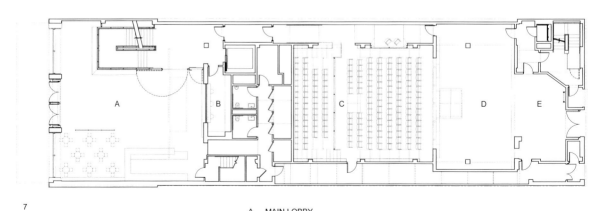

7

A MAIN LOBBY
B BOX OFFICE
C THEATER SEATING
D STAGE
E GREEN ROOM
F BLACK BOX THEATER

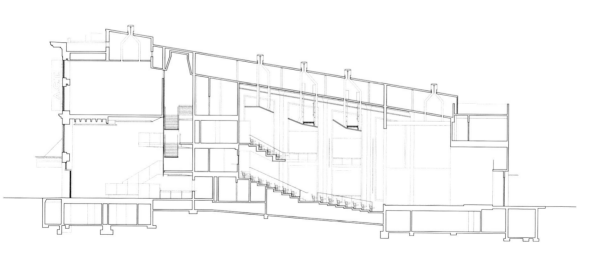

8

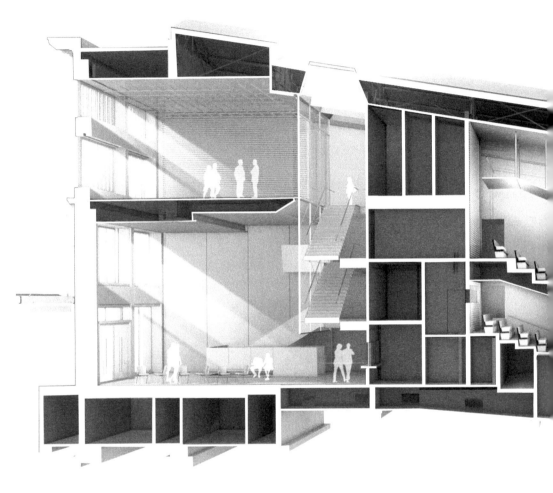

9

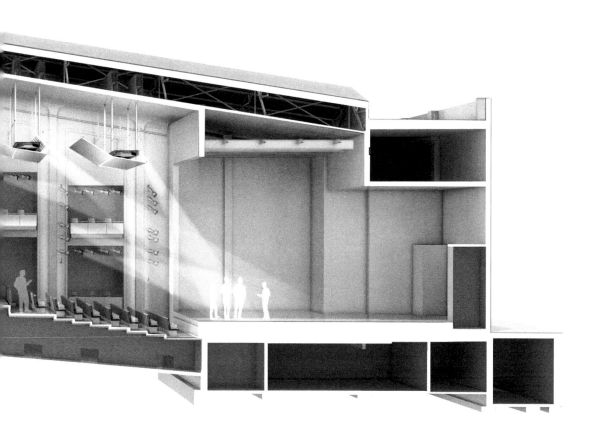

10

11

12

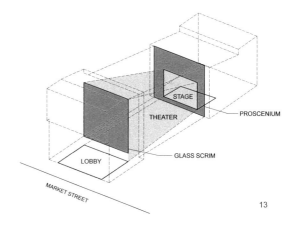

13

10 Illuminated scrim in lobby
11 Projection on scrim in lobby
12 Theater view from stage
13 Lobby/theater relationship diagram

14 Interior view rendering of black box theater
15 Atrium stair with skylight rendering

14

Saint Benedict Chapel, Sumvitg, Graubünden by Peter Zumthor

On Leadership/Authorship
A Critic's Perspective

Sarah Goldhagen

Peter MacKeith: *As we have discussed in the build-up to this conversation, your work in "situated modernisms" is compelling—not least because of your refocusing of thought in architecture away from "the usual suspects" (towards Kahn and Aalto, for instance) and more fully because your approach outlines a deeper richness and complexity to architectural practices of the mid- to late twentieth century. That said, the twinned agendas for SOM 8 and 9 assert that there is a history yet to be written that more openly and fully shifts away from the single-author emphasis in architectural practice, and instead presents significant work—even the work of Kahn and Aalto—as work of collaborative effort and a collective wisdom.*

At the least, these Journal numbers hope to open up both the popular myths of a heroic architecture and the conventional internal methodologies of professional practice. Posing these concerns as a question for your consideration within the framework of thought you have already constructed so well: does your reframing of modern architecture provide for the inclusion of such collaborative qualities and methods? Posing this as a concern even more attuned to contemporary circumstances—relative perhaps to your work as a contemporary critic: is the apparatus of appreciating and evaluating architecture—formed and promoted in schools, in the media, in award juries and in histories—long overdue for an overhaul (the recent discussion of Denise Scott-Brown's omission from Pritzker Prize recognition as a case in point)? Given the directions of the book you are working on, we are hopeful that these themes resonate with you.

Sarah Goldhagen: In my *New Republic* essay in May, 2013, on the recent initiative to (finally) recognize Denise Scott-Brown as the equally deserving recipient of the Pritzker Prize Award given in 1991 solely to Robert Venturi, I advocated for a more complex comprehension of architecture, which would include a recognition of its inherently collaborative character. As I wrote then: "… [the controversy] also raises some more provocative questions about architecture—for instance, why it continues to be an astonishingly, notoriously male-dominated profession. And, especially important in the case of Robert Venturi's Pritzker, just why its professional culture fails to recognize architecture's inherently collaborative nature. This or that individual architect—Venturi, Jean Nouvel, Zaha Hadid, whoever—gets anointed and heroized, but everybody knows that designing a building of any substantial size is such an immensely complicated undertaking that it is rarely if ever done alone."

Criticism—as opposed to academic writing, which is more forgiving—makes one acutely aware of the linguistic problems a writer grapples with when discussing architecture. Language is structured in such a way as to make it difficult not to rely, at some point, on the fiction of an individual actor. Once the critic has made this all-but-unavoidable concession, she is, like it or not, in the game of implying that a designed work has but a single author. It's a convenience, a misleading kind of shorthand we all use to describe endeavors that we full well know to be collaborative and exceedingly complex.

But this technical linguistic problem is actually a secondary issue. Many architecture critics and most architecture historians work from a critical model derived from art history, where emphasizing individual agency and artistic intention makes sense … the subjects with which art historians and art critics mostly concern themselves are individual artists, where it is usually pretty clear, at least in the basic sense, who's made what. *Les demoiselles d'Avignon* was painted by Pablo Picasso—simple. But in architecture, the primary problematic is not "one actor, or many?" but the question of *agency*, which includes not only people as individuals—clients, senior designers, junior designers, men, women, community board members—but also the larger forces shaping the design process and the built product, forces such as the phenomenological dictates of human experience, economic pressures and trends, sociological structures, and so on. With these caveats in mind, we can consider a larger question: If there is in fact a shift in the contemporary architectural moment in the paradigm of agency—from individual agency to collaborative agency—what does that paradigm shift get us? What are we to then understand with a more contemporary notion of agency?

To portray the complexity of architectural practice and product, and to devise an analytical framework adequate to that complexity, I've used the concept of "situated-ness," which I first developed while working on Louis Kahn, then expanded upon in more recent work on Alvar Aalto, and further theorize in my forthcoming book. Kahn and Aalto's work was discursively situated, meaning that through buildings they articulated a series of positions relating to the political, social, intellectual, artistic, and economic conditions of the time. Their work is also phenomenologically situated in that they designed buildings from the point of view of how users would experience them—users who inhabit bodies, bodies which live in space, stand on the ground, at a particular place, and in a specific time. These too are aspects of situated-ness in architecture that the best architects—Kahn, Aalto, Scharoun, Zumthor—have always recognized.

Analyzing and assessing the design process and built product as situated seems to me far more fruitful than approaching them as the product of a heroic maker's construction of a social vision—or worse, personal expression. Art can be an expressionistic search for identity; architecture cannot. Any designer who relies on private obsessions or dream-fueled reveries to shape design violates the essence of the vocation. To understand a building, its maker's biography is close to irrelevant. Architecture constitutes and constructs sheltering, meaningful places; situated-ness is its means. Such places, in turn, shape the social and individual lives of peoples and cities for generations. All this mandates, for users and critics, a collective sensibility, and, for makers, a deep sense of social responsibility. Institutionalizing and formalizing a collaborative paradigm of design will enable historians and critics to better portray and analyze the inherent complexity of any given architectural work—the situated constraints and opportunities, the contributions and roles of the immense number of participants involved in a work's creation and inhabitation, the multiple discourses embedded into its production.

In my forthcoming book, which is on the experience of the contemporary built environment, I operationalize this kind of expanded perspective. For example, recent research shows that men and women tend to navigate space differently—women rely more on landmarks, men on cognitive maps—which suggests that there may be a degree of inherent gender difference in the conception and production of architecture. That's a disconcerting thought, especially when most of the built environment continues to be designed and constructed by men. Such experiential issues must be included in every architect's education and professional development, no matter their gender. Exploring how people—women, men, everyone—*actually* experience the built environment will promote a deeper, more complex understanding of what architects do. The approach to complexity I am proposing for architecture is somewhat analogous to that of the psychologist and Nobel Prize winning economist Daniel

Kahneman in his *Thinking, Fast and Slow*: recognize the nature, subtleties, and illogicalities of non-conscious and conscious experience and thought, and be deliberate in how you deploy them.

There is a hard truth in this discussion, however. We can recognize complexity all we want, and in spite of our knowing better, people need specific agents, and the dictates of branding and popular culture demand them—they demand concrete figures to act as representatives of the larger collaborations and complications, on whom people can project our ambitions and values. Even the most openly collaborative architectural practices today rely upon a "public face," an articulate spokesperson, to become the face of the firm. And these people *are*

agents. They do, as individuals, make a difference in the direction of a firm or the look of a specific design.

Perhaps, then, the overarching lesson is that both individuals and the collaborative work of teams is important, and that the importance of one should not obscure the importance of the other. All our emphasis on teamwork here should not completely lay to rest the contributions of the individual. After all, when Denise Scott Brown demanded the Pritzker that she rightfully earned, she was not asking that it be given to a team, or even to her team. She wanted her agency to be recognized too, to be recognized *as an individual* and as an agent. We are all built with an inflated sense of our own agency—the final paradox is that this must be part of the equation too.

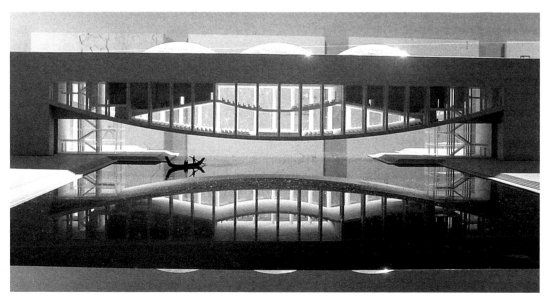

Louis I. Kahn, model for the Palazzo dei Congressi, Venice, Italy, ca. 1972. Balsawood veneer over planed birch

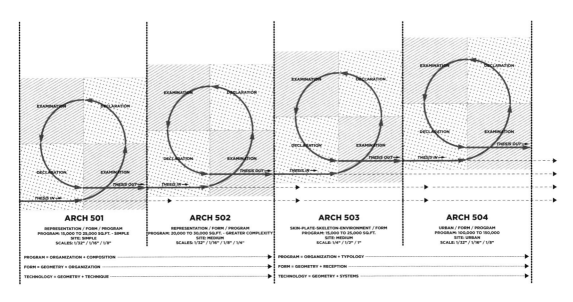

ARCH 501
REPRESENTATION / FORM / PROGRAM
PROGRAM: 15,000 TO 25,000 SQ.FT. - SIMPLE
SITE: SIMPLE
SCALES: 1/32" / 1/16" / 1/8"

ARCH 502
REPRESENTATION / FORM / PROGRAM
PROGRAM: 20,000 TO 30,000 SQ.FT. - GREATER COMPLEXITY
SITE: MEDIUM
SCALES: 1/32" / 1/16" / 1/8" / 1/4"

ARCH 503
SKIN-PLATE-SKELETON-ENVIRONMENT / FORM
PROGRAM: 15,000 TO 25,000 SQ.FT.
SITE: MEDIUM
SCALE: 1/4" / 1/2" / 1"

ARCH 504
URBAN / FORM / PROGRAM
PROGRAM: 100,000 TO 150,000
SITE: URBAN
SCALE: 1/32" / 1/16" / 1/8"

PROGRAM = ORGANIZATION + COMPOSITION
FORM = GEOMETRY + ORGANIZATION
TECHNOLOGY = GEOMETRY + TECHNIQUE

PROGRAM = ORGANIZATION + TYPOLOGY
FORM = GEOMETRY + RECEPTION
TECHNOLOGY = GEOMETRY + SYSTEMS

Rice School of Architecture's Master of Architecture Core Studio Curriculum Diagram

On Leadership/Authorship
An Educator's Perspective

Sarah Whiting

Peter MacKeith: *As an academic leader in design, you work with faculty in curriculum development and instruction, and with students, preparing them for their own trajectories in design practice. You provide moreover a framing vision for the design education of the school. How do the historical concepts of individual authorship and design leadership, as well as the more contemporary conditions of design teamwork and collaboration, enter into your discussions with faculty and students? From an academic vantage point, are these oppositional or complementary values and methods? Can such approaches and attitudes be taught and learned—and if so how? How would you describe the design studio's (understood as a central pedagogical method in design education) approaches, or understandings, of the concepts of teamwork and collaboration?*

Sarah Whiting: As with most binaries, it's the perceived *opposition* between individual authorship and collaboration that is most destructive to architecture as a discipline and as a practice (much more destructive than excessive individualism or excessive collaboration – both of which are, in fact, quite rare and usually so astonishingly uninteresting that they simply don't merit attention).

Every architect and every academic (not just in architecture but in other fields, too) knows that individual work *necessarily* feeds off of and feeds in turn the work of others, as Harold Bloom argues so well in *The Anxiety of Influence*. Poetic invention, he asserts, comes from tweaking, swerving, shifting the lineage that already exists. Intellectual invention—in poetry he claims, but we can also assert in architecture—doesn't happen *de novo*, but as a response. Collaboration needs to be understood in this broader sense. We, as academics and as architects, are in constant collaboration with others, both in real time and in what might be called disciplinary time. Finally, collaboration should not be confused with compromise. It's said that a camel is a horse designed by committee—that's the kind of disastrous compromise (*pace*, all camel aficionados!) that arises when collaboration is understood to mean that everyone has to be happy. Successful collaboration requires strong individual input. It also requires an ability to accept a strong idea from someone else and make it even stronger rather than reduce the idea via compromise.

The challenge, of course, is how to *teach* this easily misunderstood relationship between collaboration and individualism. Architecture's a fantastic field for training students to be strong individuals who constitute the strongest of collaborators, since work is done in the shared arena of the studio, discussed in the discursive arena of the seminar, and evaluated in the public arena of the pin up. Students have to be taught three things for invention, along Bloom's lines, to occur: how to have a voice of their own, how to evaluate work (their own and others'), and how to build on work (put another way, how to advance their voice). Pin ups and seminars cannot be just a moment for the professor to assess or pontificate; at the same time, they cannot be "anything goes/feel good" conversations. Students need to learn what evaluations advance a project rather than merely describe it, or even set it back. In an era where every kid in a soccer league gets a trophy, teaching students constructive criticism may well be the greatest challenge of all. While "alpha students" provide a model for the less talented (again, both in studio and seminar), all too often, lazy faculty will let their courses operate on auto pilot, giving their bit and letting the alphas run ahead, with the hope that the rest of the class will follow suit. In an environment where criticism is continuously softened or where it becomes rote, students will never establish their own voices, which means that they'll never be able to offer anything to a collaboration.

A small school is the ideal laboratory for such pedagogy. No students can hide in the wake of the alphas. No alphas can plow forward by merely repeating without advancing their projects. Everything's visible. Successful individualism and successful collaboration, in short, depends first on judgment: on evaluation and on the training of evaluation.

How do we judge in architecture? Rarely uttered, this question underlies all that we do in schools of architecture, as practitioners of architecture, and as critics of architecture. But how do we really know when a design is right? How does any one of us decide whether a building is "good" or "bad"? Does the question go unuttered because it's too obvious, or because it's anything but?

Judgment is such a weighty term—so heavy, so fraught. It provokes a bewildering aura when attention is drawn to it, like the doubt that comes when thinking too long about how to spell a word. Asking why a decision was made guarantees a frozen panic. For all of our earnest bluster, self-conscious doubts run deep in the waters of architectural production.

Judgment makes us uncomfortable because it's, well … judgmental. Open-mindedness is de rigueur for contemporary thinkers. No doubt, we have long reaped the benefits of an ever-expanding field of interdisciplinarity. New topics, voices, disciplines, geographies, and politics have exponentially multiplied, establishing a richer and more beneficial world for all of us.

To be judgmental seems utterly at odds with this expanded horizon. And yet, looking across architecture today, it strikes me that in our relentless pursuit of everything, we may have crossed the invisible line that separates proliferate good intentions from an avalanche of indiscriminacy, because while we see more, we register less.

Simultaneity has displaced singularity: ticker tapes of topics run across the bottom of every news screen; Google searches generate a multitude of answers to any given question; walkers who stumble while texting blame the obstacles rather than acknowledge that their multitasking may be putting them at risk. We're no longer held back by the assumption that you can't rub your belly and pat your head at the same time. And even if we laughingly curse this condition (too much information!), we feel more powerful for it: armed with our smartphones, we can pepper our conversations with facts, with examples, and, most importantly, with confidence.

But while this information-packed world may be long on facts, it's short on opinions. How do you pursue architecture in such a milieu? Is it a "like" tag on an early-morning surf through ArchDaily? Why "like"? Is it the project's beautifully formed concrete cantilevers? Is it the elegance of its sharply peaked form? Have you ever stopped to wonder why more than half the projects on ArchDaily every day seem to fall into one or both of those categories? Have you ever taken the time to wonder anything much about what you see there or on Archinect or Dezeen or ArchNewsNow or whatever blog or newsfeed you tune into? We're always short of time, so we surf, skim, and survey our way through all information— architecture included—daily, even hourly.

But does ever-more equate with ever-better? Has architecture advanced beyond what it was a year ago? A decade ago? A half-century ago? Have our cities become better? Have we enhanced our cultural present? Our prospective future?

At first, the abundance of information was liberating. It offered an aura of something akin to intelligence: proliferation itself became a methodology and exhaustive grew to be the obligatory qualifier for research. Labor could be measured not in hours but in the quantity of options produced. But prodigious output ought not to be mistaken for conceptual consequence. All too often, in schools as much as in offices, production is seen to be an end in itself. Far worse, the sheer multiplicity of our output might be muffling more urgently needed speculations about the future.

Architectural judgments radiate from articulated and argued discourses. Across the twentieth century these discourses included, among others, technological optimism, good-life modernism, populism, environmentalism, and, for lack of a better term, brash capitalism. If the status quo felt stifling, one could always turn the status quo on its head. Less is more not to your taste? No problem—how about less is a bore? Camps, the easiest way of identifying oneself, are also the easiest means of breaking ranks, of moving on. Camps bother us today. "I want to live here, not there," or "I want to be this, not that" has come to signal vulnerability or even incorrectness. But isn't it precisely that kind of desire, that kind of visceral subjectivity, that leads us toward a tomorrow that is better than today?

Architecture is about choices. It is about how architects negotiate the countless decisions that take place along the way from A to B: Should this room be next to that room? What is an institution? Is that factory treating its employees well? Are they part of what Paolo Virno calls the multitude? How does my project affect their individuality? How tall is a guardrail? Will this façade look good? Why am I working with this client? Will water get through there? Is concrete better than steel? Should I pay attention to context? Do I need a new font? Should that glass line up with that wall? Is that paint toxic?

That architects face a barrage of choices is nothing new, though we surely face more of them and from further corners of the world than at any previous period in history. What has changed is that they render us increasingly taciturn. We might be intentionally reserved (architects are generally more diffident than they used to be). Or we might be paralyzed (overwhelmed by so many possibilities). Or we might have succumbed to a world of clients, banks, and project managers (whose rise to significance has paralleled architecture's diminished voice). Or we might simply be more selfish than we ought to be (the world has become so, well, messy … why bother?).

Writing about this topic in the context of the *SOM Journal* is particularly poignant, given that SOM has given us some of the strongest examples of how architecture thrives most when strong voices make strong judgments and what extraordinary collaborations result. The fact that we know several SOM buildings as SOM, but also as authored by certain figures (Gordon Bunshaft, Natalie de Blois, Bruce Graham, Walter Netsch) underscores the oscillating relationship between strong voices and collaborations. Some of the best of these buildings have more than one strong voice behind them: Inland Steel (Chicago, 1958), for example, was a collaboration between Graham and Netsch; Lever House was authored by Bunshaft and de Blois. Oh to be a fly on the wall for those projects … These buildings are anything but camels.

Whatever the cause, our contemporary muteness is particularly startling when one considers the fact that architecture is intrinsically generalist. Architecture is nothing other than a means of assembling relations across its many constituent threads, threads that are never the same in any two projects. And the only hope that an architect has for making her way across this ever-changing turf is to be an expert at making decisions.

Interdisciplinarity is not a judgment—it's simply a given—an exciting given, but at this point, it's really a given. It cannot be an academic agenda; it can only be a means, but a means that has to be made strategic. For it to be effective in advancing architectural practice and discourse, it's critical that we not let interdisciplinarity become an elaborate avoidance strategy for facing judgment head on. It's our role to teach our students to "think I'll do … X, (or Y, or Z)"—to make considered judgments (not random choices) that stem from careful, close readings from within and from without our discipline. These readings take time, and take time to learn: it's also our role to construct time – to make time in our world that never has enough time.

If contemporary architecture seems complex, I'd argue that it isn't. If someone were to say that what we do is simple, I'd beg to differ. Architects decide how to add X and Y, and then to add that to Z. This is a process that is neither complicated nor simple. But it is one that takes practice: the practice of putting actual things together and the practice of thought—to echo Peter Sloterdijk—thought that potentially advances rather than simply maintains our discipline. Cultivating judgment in a school of architecture is such a practice. The practice of judgment teaches both authorship and collaboration; both a respect for history and an awareness of the present; both an expertise within the discipline and a generalist breadth. Architecture is a day-to-day life that is full of judgments. We evaluate things. We say this will be better than that, or worse than that. And then we put things together into such a way that architecture supersedes all of those individual decisions with the conviction that tomorrow will be better than today, one judgment at a time.

Walking experiment performed by the participants of The Institute for Spatial Experiments, Olafur Eliasson's five-year art academy experiment

Leadership/Teamwork in Practice, Part 2 An Interview with Helle Søholt and Olafur Eliasson

Peter MacKeith

"Leadership/Teamwork in Practice," is a constructed discussion between principal designer Helle Søholt of Gehl Architects/Urban Quality Consultants and Olafur Eliasson of Studio Olafur Eliasson focusing on their respective collaborative approaches and interdisciplinary design practices. The discussion is itself the second exercise in collaboration across the design culture, following on the previous one in SOM Journal 8, *with the ambition to draw upon the wisdom of those engaged in modes of design practice different from SOM's, either in scale of practice, or in design character altogether. The discussion is based on the belief that architecture can learn more for its sustenance from other creative fields, whether the visual arts, the literature, or design. These discussions are part of a set of comparative case studies of teamwork in design and in the related arts—urban design, film and animation production, furniture and industrial design, communications design, and strategic design.*

Peter MacKeith (PM): *Studio Olafur Eliasson and Gehl Architects as artistic and design practices both possess a strong, simple signifier as title—a firm name that seemingly identifies one individual—and are also known as interdisciplinary practices emphasizing teamwork and collaboration. Can you outline the thinking that went into the formation of the practice, even into the studio or firm name? Was a collaborative method, or at least, an interdisciplinary mentality, present from the outset?*

Helle Søholt (HS): Absolutely, we had a very collaborative approach from the very beginning of the practice. It is important to remember that when we started Jan Gehl was sixty-four years old and I was only twenty-eight. That age difference gave rise to many conversations about how to work together and how to build a practice. We knew from the start that we would focus on Jan's central urban concept of "life between buildings," but we also knew that this would never be a one-man practice. Indeed, our choice of firm name—Gehl Architects and Urban Quality Consultants—both plural—is a clear signal of our collective approach to planning and design. At the same time, we thought, if we were successful our hope and our vision was that the practice would outlive us. My ambition was always to build a team based on these collective approaches and, in fact, Jan has never signed off on drawings in the way that individual architects often do even if they have not led the design effort. Even with the age differences between Jan and myself, we have always seen ourselves as a "young" practice and, in fact, we could say more to the point, a contemporary practice. In contemporary terms this means that we are very aware of the relative age of many of our employees and indeed many of the people with whom we collaborate outside of the office. To put it even more specifically, we are working within a Generation Y world and Generation Y expects to be involved and empowered in their design roles.

As to the origins as a practice, at the time we began Jan had had a forty-year career as an academic in urban design research and in heading an Urban Design Research Group at the Royal Academy here in Copenhagen. My ambition was to apply that research practically. So, just as Jan worked in that research group, all projects begin with a careful and thorough study of that project city and urban condition. Thus, on the one hand we have continued that academic approach and we feel have successfully transferred it to the realities of urban life; however, we still develop our methods and our tools and what I would call our method of design leadership. But throughout our development we have maintained the ethos of "life between buildings"—of a focus on the people who inhabit cities and who are active citizens in their cities. It could be said in fact that "Gehl" signifies

An early test for *Your Rainbow Panorama* on the studio roof top.

"design for people" … this is our brand, beyond the person who possesses that name, such that the Gehl practice means "people in design," and a sustainable approach to urban design.

Olafur Eliasson (OE): The studio grew out of a desire to make art. If a certain project requires a specialized skill, then we look for an appropriate person to do that. People have been brought in for their individual expertise, so the make up of the studio is a reflection of the artworks and exhibitions that we have worked on here. It has gradually expanded to include everything from skilled craftsmen, art handlers, filmmakers, and trained architects and engineers to programmers, archivists, art historians, cooks, and a geometer. Many of the core people have worked with me since the early years, but the studio's boundaries are also relatively open, with people coming and going, so some people who work for

me also sometimes work for other people or on their own. If you take a particularly complex project, like the façades of Harpa Reykjavik Concert Hall and Conference Centre, for example, this required an in-house team of architects, led by Sebastian Behmann, with whom I have worked since 2001. Einar Thorsteinn, also a longtime collaborator, developed the geometry behind the quasi-brick, the module we used to construct the façades. And there are a number of other people working together with Sebastian and myself on various architectural projects, from complex geometrical forms to large-scale installations like Double Sunrise, in the Interpipe factory in Dnepropetrovsk, Ukraine, to Cirkelbroen, a bridge that will open in Copenhagen in the next few months.

Similarly, the archive is actually more of a proactive entity, concerned with knowledge production, than a reactive, backward-looking archive in the traditional sense. As we mine the potential of this approach, the

City-telling tools. Gehl Architects uses many types of physical tools, such as Lego® bricks and people, to engage their clients and collaborators in imagining and prototyping the qualities of people-friendly cities, through their workshops and master classes.

archive continues to grow and expand to new fields, like social media, publications, and filmmaking. It has become more and more capable of standing on its own to the point where it might be misleading to refer to it as an archive at all.

In general, I want everyone in my studio team to have a very strong sense of co-responsibility for the work. I retain the key artistic decisions, of course, but at some point, I can leave certain decisions to others. For this to be possible, it's necessary for them to understand the principles behind the works. As people working at the studio become more sensitive to what is essential in the works, they become more autonomous. If I can involve people sufficiently in the work, then their job performance will inspire me in return.

PM: *With a long record of diverse accomplishments, Gehl Architects holds an established place in the design culture. Olafur, with a record of diverse accomplishments—across many scales and locales—your work holds an established place in art, architecture, and design culture. What do you think are the attributes that can be ascribed to the work achieved under the Eliasson or Gehl name, despite the range of work and the range of designers, collaborators, and assistants employed? How are those attributes maintained across the studio or the practice, across the range of designers, participants, work, and locations … as the firm has grown and attracted more and different projects?*

HS: What is different for us—from a normal architectural practice—is that we are working with cities, with all the urban challenges and complexities of the contemporary city: densification, housing, infrastructure, etc. We are working always with both the quality of the existing city and with the pressure of new developments. When you are advising on such essential issues and specifically on the quality of life for citizens in any city, we believe it must be a collaborative process. For us co-creation is a fundamental principle: we work with cities, with civic leadership, in constant evaluation and discussion, we work with cities and civic leadership to build their capacity for sustainable urban design and we are working to empower those cities and their leadership and their citizens to address these issues and these complexities on their own terms.

We have worked in fifty-seven cities in the last five years. We see only increasing demand for urban design quality across the world. But our ambitions for our practice are not driven by size or number of projects. Rather, our ambitions are motivated by this vision of capacity building and empowerment and thought-leadership. By these terms, I mean the enabling of municipalities to understand themselves and to lead themselves through the support and advice that we can give by virtue of our research and experience. To paraphrase an old adage, we do not give people fish, we teach people how to fish for themselves. Our practice in many ways is again fundamentally collaborative and participatory; we organize lectures, workshops, seminars, and design reviews wherever we are commissioned so that everyone—all stakeholders and all citizens—gain power to determine their own urban futures.

Earlier I mentioned our understanding of ourselves as a young and contemporary practice, as well as a practice that relies on a team-based approach to the cities in which we are commissioned. It takes particular qualities in each of our employees in order for this team-based collaborative approach to be credible and successful. To work within our practice all team members must have three fundamental abilities: 1) leadership skills applicable across cultures, that is to say a person who is confident in the practice's collective knowledge and method, who is aware of the depth of the Gehl research, and who can transmit that knowledge with confidence in many settings; 2) care (not arrogance), that is to say an ability to listen and to be culturally aware in all places, to engage people with diverse interests and ambitions, using the Gehl "toolbox" of method and analysis to arrive at innovative solutions particular to the specific urban locale; and 3) optimism; a certain belief that you can build a better place. We work in the sincere belief that even in the worst places there is always an opportunity to do good. I would add only to this trio of qualities that in many ways these are not qualities that can be taught and therefore our interview process for prospective employees is always very thorough and in-depth.

I lead by advice and suggestion and always with an emphasis on collaboration. We are a knowledge company and it is important that we share our knowledge among each other. We spend a lot of time in discussion of both project and approaches because we need to be consistent in what we mean when we are working with our teams across cities and time zones and geographies. There are several ways that we try to attain this consistency of internal knowledge. For instance, four times every year we have what we call "knowledge days" … we close the office, we choose a theme, we discuss it thoroughly as an office and we try to come to mutual understandings of that theme. Almost weekly, at the same time, there will be lunchtime presentations of our own work to each other. I could say that we are in continuous discussion in the knowledge that there is never just one solution, but pushing to identify new ways of establishing sustainable urban cultures. Both inside the practice and in the work we do with cities and citizens we will often say that the method is more about learning than deciding.

OE: It's not about maintaining a certain aesthetic or attributes, but about how we approach a certain question set —questions about the co-production of space, about movement, responsibility, perception. I, together with my studio, explore these questions in various media and situations that, in turn, color the questions and their possible answers (thinking, doing, thinking, doing . . .). These can be questions about the production of space— whether public, architectural, or other—about compassion, about being with others, experiencing on one's own and with others. In that sense, I view the works as experimental setups rather than as static objects.

In response to your questions about collaboration, I would like to emphasize that an artwork is always a collaboration when encountered by the viewer. The artwork's meaning is produced by the situation it enters once it leaves the studio, by the people who view it, and the context in which it is exhibited or used.

PM: *How would you describe the Studio Eliasson or Gehl Architects approach, or understanding, of the concepts of teamwork and collaboration? Relative to the parallel ideas of individual authorship, or even "design leadership," what role does teamwork and collaboration play in the conception and realization of a typical project? If it is a central value or method, how is it encouraged, nurtured, or reinforced? Are there incentives to an emphasis on such approaches? Are there also disadvantages?*

HS: Knowledge sharing in the way I just described has its challenges, as almost all of us were brought up within a hierarchical system of knowledge sharing. One teacher always presenting to many students. The question for us as a practice—and then as a question for our civic partners—is how to capture individual knowledge and experience and make it organizational knowledge and collective experience. The process here of knowledge sharing among many participants may, in fact, lead to a certain slowness in decision making. But, if you weigh that slowness against the depth of knowledge that you are achieving relative to the absolute quality that you are achieving, we believe that slowness is a worthy cost.

Alongside this slowness in collective knowledge sharing there is also the fact that professional relationships are almost always personal as well … clients are used to having personal, individual relationships with consultants. But our best work with cities has been when city leaders understand our team approach—understand that we will always send our best person for that particular moment in the process. This approach is a bit controversial in current conventional practice where an account manager is the norm in client relationships. But in our view, given the complexities of urban design, our team members can be specifically tuned to issues of housing, or data collection, or survey method, or infrastructure analysis … and that that team member can be the appropriate and necessary Gehl representative at a particular moment in the process. This for us is shared wisdom and team-based consulting. There are dual expectations here: the client has to trust our method and our team and we have to deliver consistent professionalism and quality deliverables.

Today at Gehl we are seven partners. Three partners manage internal teams and four manage external projects and all are of equal value and presence in the overall direction of the practice. Our internal work requires the balancing of individual egos with the larger goals of the practice. Individual ambitions are admirable, but in our work knowledge sharing and mutual respect is essential.

As I said earlier, we are different from a normal architecture practice. Our professional focus is on the city and the city needs its own signature to the work that is being undertaken. The work that we do will ultimately be their work. As consultants we support the city and sometimes we are given credit and sometimes not. Simply put, we advise the city, but it is the city that is credited with authorship. As we work with citizens and social groups and municipal leadership, this end result of authorship is made very clear. We clash more often with author-centered architects rather than with civic leaders and so we seek collaborators who understand this reasoning.

OE: I would say that one of the main criteria by which people today judge the success of an artwork is the work's perceived precision. Many often think that success and precision lie, on the one hand, in the idea for the work of art and then, on the other, in the finished work of art. For me, the important thing is the precision with which a team addresses an idea and carries it from thought to artwork. Teamwork is highly relevant to the success of a work of art today, the actual process of working with a team, the precise synchronization of the team, the sense of trajectory. When you make something precise, it is this path, the way an idea is rendered into a work of art, that is the key to its precision and its success. It is how the precision is performed.

So the entire structure of the studio exists to help turn thinking into doing, to help create new realities. Of course it is helpful to have a community of trusted people around with whom I can discuss my ideas as I develop them—think better in a group—but it goes even deeper than

this: it is actually difficult for me to judge an object's potential when I look at it by myself. Objects are social constructs. Their meanings are produced in-between people, in groups. I might look at something on my own and find it uninspiring, but as soon as I stand there and look at the object together with somebody else, I become interested in the thing and can better form ideas about it. In a sense, I see the object through the other person's presence.

Also when I'm working with other people, I feel temporality and the passing of time in a much stronger way. And this awareness of time makes me much more active. I'm simply much more efficient when working with others than when I am working alone.

PM: *You have also taught with an academic appointment and work with student-interns, preparing them for professional practice or for their own artistic practices. How do the concepts of teamwork and collaboration (again, relative to individual authorship and design leadership) enter into your discussions with students? Can such approaches and attitudes be taught and learned—and, if so, how?*

HS: There are immense challenges in schools of design. We need both creative thinkers and collaborative leaders entering the design professions. Architects, and especially urban designers, are becoming facilitators of change through design—but this role is most powerfully realized by being creators of collaborations. Again, many of these qualities that tend toward collaboration and knowledge sharing are not necessarily ones that can be taught, but equally they are also not ones that are being taught. I think students could be out much more in the "real world" while they are still in school, in situations of social engagement—involved, for instance, in local government. It's true that schools can be bounded, ideal places: "free zones" for thinking and intellectual preparation. This ideal precinct of the university is hugely important for a designer's development. But I also believe that a good student designer can develop an awareness of real processes, of real conditions, of the pragmatism needed for real solutions. I believe a level of pragmatism can and should be learned because the world is not ideal and we need to have the combination of optimism and pragmatism in our toolbox in order to work effectively.

We believe that we can make a few exemplary projects, but the means to do this will always be by balancing many viewpoints.

OE: I should also mention that I collaborate on teaching with two colleagues, Eric Ellingsen and Christina Werner, who are deeply involved in all levels of the Institut für Raumexperimente, from organizing and programming events to initiating discussions, experiments, exhibitions, publications, and walks.

It is surprising to think that although much teaching actually goes on in a group, people often overlook the fact that it is often the very situation of being in the group that is more educational than the information that the teacher has to convey. So while I do not necessarily directly encourage teamwork or even collaboration among my students, I do think we teach ourselves through being with other people, by sharing ideas and speaking with others, and simply thinking in the presence of others. I find that students often learn most just from the experience of being together in a group, trying to make their ideas reality, trying to communicate to one another. So you could say that, for me, teaching itself is a very collaborative process, in which the teacher is only one player on the field.

Gehl Study Tours are a platform for inspiring dialogue, engaging experts, and seeing relevant urban challenges first hand. In this case, Copenhagen is the living laboratory, and the Gehl team uses the day to cycle around the city, stop-off at pre-arranged locations, and learn more about retail's impact on the urban environment.

Frontispiece of *Essai sur l'Architecture,* by Marc-Antoine Laugier, Paris, 1755.

Agency and Authorship
An Interview with John Harwood

Peter MacKeith

Peter MacKeith (PM): *In a recent published discussion with political economist Jonathan Levy, you explore the idea of "capital as subject" as a question with particular relevance to architecture, "especially as architectural firms have, since the end of the nineteenth century, transmogrified themselves into vast corporations in their own right after the models of managerial corporate enterprises and financial consultancies, viz., Arup, SOM, and so forth." I appreciate the line of thought (mediation, representation, abstraction) you pursue in this regard, but could you also contemplate a parallel line of consideration—of the effect that this "transmogrification" has had upon the myths and realities of contemporary architectural production and the process by which design decisions are made? This transformation of professional practice has been in motion since World War II, but neither the general public nor many architectural historians seem to fully recognize it. What happens to ideas of "leadership" and "authorship" in this transformation?*

John Harwood (JH): As I understand the question, you are referring to the persistence of the managerial mythology of "decision-making": that an individual is the one making the decisions in any meaningful sense. On this mythology—long since deconstructed not only by humanists, philosophers, and critical theorists, but by the capitalists, economists, and scientists who have produced the vast improvisational "complex" we live with today of multinational corporations, state bureaucracies, "networks," and "markets"—rests the entire living and breathing anachronism of the (strong) author. The individual—which is usually a kind of biopolitical shorthand for "a single human being"—does indeed make decisions, of course: what to put on her toast in the morning, what to say to the bank representative when he cannot pay his credit card bill, and so on. Such quotidian decisions, however, are very highly constrained. There are only so many things one can put on toast, one must be able to afford those things, some corporate body must have produced and marketed the condiment in the first place, and so on. These constraints are technically, economically, and socially produced.

It is equally clear that when such an individual works as a "decision maker" or "leader," even as a CEO or head of state, his or her capacity to make a decision about any given matter is equally or more constrained. Anyone who has ever been put "in charge" of something knows this in his or her bones. Seen in this light, one might think with at least some small degree of sympathy of the cold war president or general with his finger on the proverbial red button, or of the businessman who makes a decision between laying off workers or seeing investors' shares plummet, even if one's true sympathies lie with the workers. In other words, since Adam Smith, or at the very least since the formulation of theoretical management tools such as game theory and operations research, there should no longer be any history that takes the actions of individuals as its core data set. That's not history, that's biography. This, of course, is all a rather crude gloss on many and much more nuanced arguments about the nature of power.

One might come at this problem from another direction, which is that of the metaphor of "agency." When one is an agent, meaning a person possessing agency, one has a tendency to assume against all evidence that this means that one possesses "power over a situation." Being an agent, of course, means quite the opposite. If one is a citizen, one is an agent of the state; if one is an insurance agent, one is a servant of a corporation; if one is a travel agent, one makes someone else's travel plans on behalf of a company. It doesn't really matter whether or not one desires to perform the tasks required, only that one fulfills them.

So there is a profound problem, in my view, for the architect and historian in all of this. It is plain that, while the actions of individuals are choices and that those choices are meaningful to the individuals who make them, they cannot produce of themselves the raw data out of which

Babbitt, Sinclair Lewis, 1922

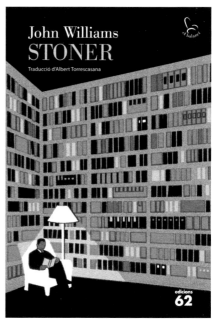

Stoner, John Williams, 1965

one might formulate a design or a historical narrative. And worse, viewed through the lens of a given design problem or historical narrative, the individual decisions once held so sacred by some turn out to be largely insignificant. The choices themselves should in these instances be seen as insufficient causes, because the intricate web of causality of which they are a part does not allow the designer or the historian to attribute special status to those choices as a sufficient cause of a "larger" design scheme or historical event.

In my own very small contribution as an architectural historian to thinking about this problem in new ways, my focus has been on effecting a very simple methodological inversion. By deferring our evaluation of the individual decision (although these can later be very useful in defining details), and instead attempting first a description of a corporate situation, we can sidestep the entire question of authorship (at least momentarily, since subject-verb-object grammar and discourse have a way of pulling us right back into the mythology) and get on with the business of seeing complex historical events as the products of the interactions between (rather than "decisions" of) complex, non-monolithic aggregations of human endeavor. After all, what is a corporation if not an initially and constantly improvised (and in a very real sense fictional) superstructure produced to allow human beings to collaborate as something other than a group of individuals?

The transformation of architectural authorship that I and many other historians working today are attempting to trace has certainly been accelerating since World War II; however, one can and should see this transformation dialectically, in a very long process that we can trace back to the late Middle Ages, and has been undergoing transformation since. That we can see from where we are, in an age we tend to call "advanced" or "global" capitalism, that a simplistic view of authorship is insufficient to describe our own world, actually brings us very close to a problem that would have been familiar to artists, art critics, and scholars in the Italian Renaissance.

The Power Elite, C. Wright Mills, 1956

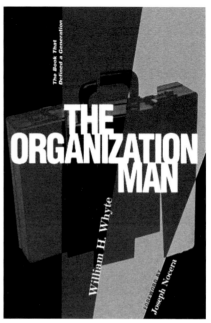

The Organization Man, William H. Whyte, 1956

PM: *A background reference shared between SOM 8 and 9 has been Hitchcock's essay, "The Architecture of Bureaucracy and the Architecture of Genius." It was also reprinted not too long ago in the pages of* Hunch, *with a very good introduction by Joan Ockman, and you examine this essay at some length in an upcoming issue of* Perspecta. *There is a surprisingly contemporary quality to his premises, I think. The contradictions he sought to resolve still seem to be present today—perhaps in a more subtle (even insidious) manner, if I understand you correctly: a Silicon Valley headquarters actually conceals its "bureaucratic" operations behind a mask of "transparency, flexibility and playfulness," and its "corporate" character is validated by an artistic act of "genius" design. Does Hitchcock need updating, given the radical shifts of economics, technology, and culture? What might be the salient points of commentary in such a revisitation?*

JH: I think that you are absolutely right that Hitchcock's

essay has had a long afterlife—and I also agree that it has a profound contemporary relevance. In my essay for *Perspecta* I tried to explain exactly why Hitchcock's essay, and another from the nineteen-forties, John Summerson's "The Mischievous Analogy," continue to trouble those of us in architectural culture who have any sense of the vast problems and lacunae that face the architect and architectural historian when it comes to understanding the corporation and its significance for contemporary architectural practice. In brief, my argument runs something like this:

At the end of World War II, architectural historians simply stopped talking about the nature of the corporation and its influence on architectural production as such. Even the historians putatively most committed to the materialist notion of architecture as a superstructural product of basic economic conditions—such as Manfredo Tafuri—did not, and perhaps could not, tackle this crucial question. Hitchcock's essay, appearing as it did in 1947 in the pages of the Architectural Review, became something like a "last word" on these matters. This despite the fact that Hitchcock's essay was in fact conjectural and projective. He believed he was seeing, and therefore predicting, a transformation in architectural production that perhaps threatened the quality of architectural design as such, in which the conventional architectural practice had or would split into three wholly different modes of architectural activity: the conventional architect (or small-scale firm) who produced buildings for large-scale organizations; the newly emergent architectural firm that operated at the level of what we would today call the multinational corporation (Hitchcock cites the examples of Albert Kahn, Inc. and SOM); and a mysterious third way, held out as a mere possibility rather than a fait accompli, "the architecture of genius." These categories and the terms associated with them, albeit with slight adjustments, remain in use today—especially in surveys of, say, twentieth-century architecture in architecture schools, where after three lectures on Le Corbusier, one gets one lecture that lumps together pre-WWII factory architecture, Art Deco and postwar office building architecture, and some of TAC's more unsavory buildings. Most students are lucky if World War II appears as anything more than a conspicuous absence separating one lecture on Corbu from the next.

But it is essential, in my view, to note that Hitchcock's was a rear-guard action, intended to salvage for architecture the anachronistic notion of a strong author by appealing to various unique and personal styles of design which could never be assimilated by a faceless corporate structure. Needless to say, Hitchcock's exemplary genius was Frank Lloyd Wright, who appears as an "organic" *deus ex machina* to resolve (perhaps) the threat of corporate design bleeding architecture dry of all of its "art." It is telling, though, that Hitchcock chose to illustrate the essay with a photograph of the as-yet-unfinished design for the Guggenheim; perhaps he was less confident than he sounded at first read that the geniuses could carry the day.

PM: *An obvious focus in your book* The Interface, *and for others working in architectural history today, is the presence and development of information/digital technologies in contemporary culture, and their transformational effects—in the built environment and in architecture as a practice. You describe IBM early in* The Interface *as a "determining case" in the self-articulation of corporate character, so fundamental was its identification with not just the technologies but the potentials and effects of those technologies. Others examining contemporary practice indicate that these technologies are now upending the historical, conventional hierarchies of architectural practice—of "authorship," "ownership," and "knowledge." Do you agree with this assessment? If so, is there a "determining case" that can be identified in contemporary architecture practice, one that is now self-articulating a more aware and productive mode of practice based on the potentials of these technologies? Or are there other models to be sought for architectural practice—do these technologies, in fact, potentially lead away from the corporate model of organization?*

JH: I am a historian, so I tend to be rather uncomfortable with contemporary criticism, predictions, and futurologies. But it is true that many are now concerned with fundamental and pressing questions about the effects of certain technologies on the basic conditions of architectural practice today. And, of course, since all histories end in the present in one way or another, I am concerned with these same questions.

Perhaps I can answer your question this way, without seeming to be too cagey: I do believe that we are seeing, with the increasingly integrated use of computational technologies in contemporary architectural practice, more of what we have seen. In its whole-hearted embrace of the computer, architectural culture has guaranteed several things will continue to take place at least for the time being. One is the accelerating transformation of the architectural academy into a place for the experimental application of basic and marketing research into computational technologies and their peripherals. What was

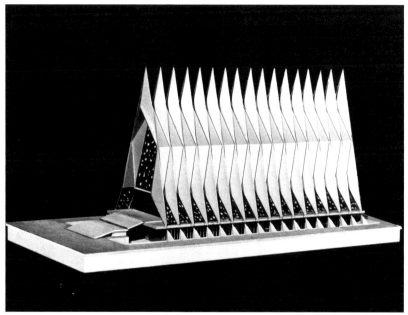

United States Air Force Academy Cadet Chapel model, SOM, 1963

Solomon R. Guggenheim Museum model, Frank Lloyd Wright, 1959

once the province of a handful of boutique, shoestring operations at MIT funded by larkish grants from multi-national high-tech corporations is now the modus operandi of almost every ambitious school of architecture: give us the gear, we will tinker with it and then show you what we can do. I am not intending to communicate a value judgment one way or another about this state of affairs (even if it is true that I wish that other important architectural activities received as much or more attention from faculty and students alike), but I think it is a statement that bears repetition.

Another is the continued application of the surface as the primary conditioning concept of contemporary architectural practice (and architects are most definitely not alone here). We have moved from a situation in which the panel and graphic interfaces of the nineteen-fifties and sixties were a major innovation in the industrial design of computers, which was not yet quite understood, to a situation in which any knowledge whatsoever not only can but must be figured as a surface. (I am a particular admirer of the geographer and architect John May's work on this subject.) This extends not only to the notion of the reduction of computational interfaces to more or less elegant surfaces; it is a matter of architects thinking of what they do as a matter of reading, manipulating, and producing surfaces. GIS, BIM, and of course "three-dimensional" modeling and fabrication applications (I have to side with Panofsky here, there is nothing more resolutely two-dimensional!), and so on, although we should perhaps not leave out software for handling costings, structural simulations, and logistics—all of these surficial technologies are now the primary tools of architectural design, and will as such guarantee the ultimate surficiality of architecture's products.

Lastly, we are in—but have yet to come to terms with—a situation today where the corporate nature of architectural production is unavoidable. There is little sense, from my point of view, in imagining that today any architect or architectural historian is producing whatever it is that he or she is producing in a "non-corporate" context. One doesn't need to be paranoid to understand that.

Everywhere we look, we are surrounded and subsumed by corporations: the state (in the US, we have multiple states, at the municipal, county, state, and federal levels!), voluntary organizations, professional organizations, schools, businesses, and so on.

When it comes to the technologies that you ask about, since these are produced and distributed (only and always) by corporations, and whenever used they are used for or regulated by corporations, they inevitably lead their users further into the corporate model of organization. I agree with Reinhold Martin, there is no "outside" to this condition at present. The corporate condition is absolutely intrinsic to architecture, not just as it exists in capitalism, but as a discursive, disciplined body of knowledge that is technical and social before it becomes itself. Whenever I am tempted to forget this, I return to Book II, chapter I of Vitruvius, and his foundational myth of the discipline. There the lightning strikes the tree—matter transmuted into energy, Prometheus alighting on the surface of the mortal plane, fire in hand—and as a result, per Morris Hickey Morgan's translation: "After [the furious flame] subsided, they drew near, and observing that they were very comfortable standing before the warm fire, they put on logs and, while thus keeping it alive, brought up other people to it, showing them by signs how much comfort they got from it.… Therefore it was the discovery of fire that originally gave rise to the coming together of men, to the deliberative assembly, and to social intercourse." The mimetic faculty and shelters come next. The structure and sequence is simple, and it cannot be reversed: technology, language, sociability, corporate organization, architecture.

To return to the mid-twentieth century for a moment, I will conclude with two brief anecdotes. In his 1940 book on the practice of the still relatively young profession of industrial design, Harold Van Doren explained—using some cartoonish but compelling diagrams—that the only way to preserve a modicum of autonomy in one's work for a corporate client (he called them "companies") was not to join the corporation, but rather become immanent to the corporation. If the designer was active in consulting with every aspect and part of a corporation, rather than taking up a small role in one or another corner of the tree diagram of the corporate hierarchy, then the designer's agency was expansive and productive. I think that this piece of advice remains worthy of consideration today.

And lastly, it was SOM's founding partner and first "catalyst," Nathaniel Owings, who looked at his own corporation and wondered in his first memoir: "What had we become? Certainly not designers in the classic sense. We were entrepreneurs, promoters, expediters, financiers, diplomats; we were men of too many trades and masters of none." I think if one reads that brief passage today without the taint of nostalgia or regret, and instead accepts that the architectural profession really has changed in fundamental ways, then it is a bit easier to get on with imagining what a better mode of corporate architectural practice would look like.

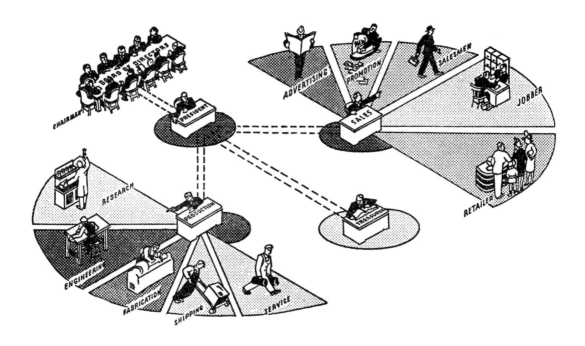

Harold van Doren's organizational diagram from *Industrial Design: A Practical Guide,* 1940

Gordon Bunshaft, 1909-1990

Gordon Bunshaft:
What Convinces Is Conviction

Nicholas Adams

"... just plain folks like we are."[1]

Few architects have had a more fortuitous entrance into the profession than Gordon Bunshaft (1909–1990). He returned from World War II to a job with a firm that had thrived in his absence, proving itself in large construction projects for the government. He designed for a society keen for his vision and with a pair of bosses willing to allow him the freedom to design to his own exacting standards. Is the rest just history, or was the career of Gordon Bunshaft a model for how a person can adapt over time, demonstrating different modes of leadership in new situations?

Gordon Bunshaft was, of course, a man defined by the era in which he lived and worked. He behaved like a titan of industry, a decisive army general, an architectural John Wayne. His gruff manner, silences, and staccato syllogistic explanations are remembered vividly by those who knew him.[2] Bunshaft's comments were terse. He had come up with the rational solution; discovered the missing element a program needed; decided what the client wanted; or, at any rate, what the client now understood he required. There was no call for him to say more. These were fortuitous times—there were SOM salesmen who loved the limelight, and modern architecture seemed to speak for itself: Bunshaft remained silent. For a decade or more, indeed, it was the kind of architecture that everyone wanted. Gordon Bunshaft was SOM's one and only design partner until 1960.

Gordon Bunshaft took his name and reputation, founded on the skin and bones of Lever House (1952), Manufacturers Trust (1954), and Chase Manhattan (1961), and developed a new architecture of concrete. He listened and questioned and learned. He was still gruff, occasionally crude, prone to pipe-sucking silences, pushing questions away with the same brief answers: it had to be done; it was the logical solution; it offered an opportunity we couldn't pass up. Though he was no longer the only design partner at SOM and often scorned his fellow partners, Bunshaft was its acknowledged leader. He joked that the only reason his name was not on the masthead was that then the initials of the firm would be S.O.B.[3]

When the headwinds grew stronger in the nineteen-seventies Bunshaft was still Bunshaft, a difficult person who spoke little, wrote less, and who delivered personal judgments that cut to the quick, fighting a rear-guard action to keep postmodernism at bay.[4] He was still pushing questions off at arm's length, where they would be left to die. As he came to the end of his career at SOM, some thought having outstayed his welcome, Bunshaft could still rise to challenges, seeking out younger employees when it suited him, producing original work that often received high praise. And then he was gone—retired in 1979 and dead eleven years later.

Bunshaft left behind remarkably little beyond his buildings. There are a few drawings in his hand, mostly from his student days, very few alternative schemes to show how he thought through problems, no essays or lectures, and the surviving interviews reveal only the familiar staccato. The destruction of his house on Long Island (1963) in 2008 removed the last vestige of his personal life that might have been picked over for clues, and the Museum of Modern Art has dispersed much of the art collection he gave them. His family—there were no children—is unwilling to talk on the record about this complicated man. So to understand how he stayed on top—and to evaluate what he meant to the firm that never bore his name—we are left to talk with people who knew the public Bunshaft and to study the correspondence he left behind.

Of course it was the times. When he returned to SOM after World War II, cultural tastes had begun to form around modern architecture, pushed by the Museum of Modern Art and sustained by wealthy patrons, advocated in magazines, and appreciated by a generation that wanted to turn their back on the prewar ways. So a firm that could make it its business to offer something new was itself newsworthy. "Skid's Boys"—as they were

Grout Elementary, Schenectady, New York

referred to in *Fortune* magazine, in 1958—purportedly embodied the kind of selfless teamwork that had licked the Germans and defeated the Japanese; an office without individual will, wholly in tune with the wishes of its clients and the country, each employee a perfect demonstration of William H. Whyte's "organization man."[5] The fact that SOM did not release the names of its designers and advertised itself as "design by committee" or "design by conference," made the firm an architectural reflection of corporate culture, that favored the social ethic of the group.[6] In the catalogue for the Museum of Modern Art exhibition of 1950 celebrating their work—a special honor as it was the first exhibition at the museum dedicated to the work of one firm (as opposed to an individual architect)—SOM was presented as being animated by two disciplines: "the discipline of modern architecture and the discipline of American organizational methods."[7] Bunshaft must have gone along with this approach when he came back after the war. But a decade or more later, and shortly after the appearance of the *Fortune* magazine article, it had begun to grate on him. A year later, in *Newsweek*, Bunshaft denied the notion that there was

something called "design by committee. There always has to be one dominant force, someone who comes up with the original design." Later in the same article he was quoted as saying: "I'm in charge of design. The other partners also participate in designing, but by criticism."[8] His fellow partners censured him for these comments.

Despite this, he was indispensable and the partners wanted him, perhaps they needed him. Well adapted to the times as he was, they allowed Bunshaft to establish a common standard for design for the whole firm. He was very good. The English architect John Winter (b. 1930) describes meeting Bunshaft at the San Francisco office in 1958. Winter had been working for weeks on an intractable problem (Bank of America, Sacramento) and "heard that the great Gordon Bunshaft was coming out from the New York office to visit. Word quickly went round the office and we were all very excited. I had expected just a tough businessman and not much more than that but when he arrived he was so impressive. I showed him my Sacramento project and explained the problem. He got out his pencil and with a few scribbles in thirty seconds he solved the whole thing."[9] As his senior

Wyeth Laboratories, Radnor Township, Pennsylvania

CBS Lab and Technical Center, Stamford, Connecticut

designer Roger Radford (SOM 1953–90) commented: "... I suppose the dominance that Bunshaft exerted in New York ... meant that really all the buildings of any ... consequence had his stamp."[10] To the list of thirty-eight buildings that Bunshaft claimed as his own, add those where his influence or intervention cannot be doubted: it just *looks* like Bunshaft was there.[11]

To these, then, add some of the designs from across the country undertaken by other offices.[12] Some of these interventions are well-known, such as Inland Steel, Chicago (1957) or the Air Force Academy, Colorado Springs (1958); some are less well known, such as the Veterans Memorial Coliseum, Portland (1957). Even buildings where there is no evidence that he gave an opinion, such as the Crown-Zellerbach Building, San Francisco (1959), depend on Bunshaft—which is to say that within SOM he was freely acknowledged as the creator of its vernacular. Not the vernacular of the innocent or the untrained, not just a modernist vernacular, but a firm-wide vernacular. In 1960, *Architectural Forum* published an article illustrating prototypical SOM detailing. Entitled "Details of Distinction," the article documented ceilings, window walls, and door frames from Bunshaft's major buildings: Union Carbide, Connecticut General, Manufacturers Trust, Lever House, Reynolds Metal Corporation. The article also included buildings not traditionally associated with Bunshaft but where he—or his associates—had a significant influence: Inland Steel, Chicago (Walter Netsch, Bruce Graham, 1957), the Hartford Fire Insurance Building, Chicago (Bruce Graham with Natalie de Blois, 1961) and Warren Petroleum, Tulsa (Bruce Graham, 1957). "From these detailed studies," the author notes, "emerges a finished building that holds few surprises—excepting the surprise of seemingly effortless perfection."[13] And there was Ezra Stoller's particular style of photographing Bunshaft buildings that the other partners wanted for their buildings, a style that conspired to make buildings that were not identical, look similar.

If the nineteen-fifties made Bunshaft's reputation (and allowed him to think his reputation might eclipse the firm for which he worked), the second and third decades demonstrated his ability to change, something neither his early career nor his personality prepares one to expect. There were new tastes to be accommodated.[14] In April 1954 Bunshaft commented on the future of architecture:

Corning Glass offices, New York City

"Why should we be in such a rush to abandon rectangular buildings? Why don't we build a few good ones?"[15] Less than four years later, in January 1958, Nathaniel Owings assured an interviewer: "This firm is not stuck with the 'stainless-steel standard,' as our competition calls it. We're interested in plasticity, and we're exploring every avenue to get it."[16] Whether it was Mies with Seagram or Le Corbusier at Ronchamp and Chandigarh, or the maturing of Bruce Graham and Walter Netsch in Chicago and Chuck Bassett in San Francisco—a thousand flowers bloomed. The quest for change required a response from the gruff master. The years of collaboration with Paul Weidlinger (1914–1999) not only produced a new kind of architecture but also a new Bunshaft. Leon Moed (SOM 1954–91) recalls that this form of collaboration required different qualities from Bunshaft. The imperative of change obligated him to adopt the interrogative. The technologies of the curtain wall were well known to him. He might press here or there, but he knew roughly what was possible and what was not possible.

CIL (Telus) Montreal, Quebec

Banco de Bogotá, Bogotá, Colombia

But concrete was another matter. In the nineteen-fifties, Bunshaft postponed extensive consultation with engineers until the design was well advanced, but with Weidlinger, he recognized the desirability of early coordination: "We knew we could do all sorts of things using concrete . . . but we needed education. As soon as we got some rough ideas, the senior designer and Paul and I—mostly Paul and I—would get together. Sometimes Paul would say, 'You can't do this,' but he never made design suggestions."[17] Leon Moed who worked closely with Bunshaft from the late nineteen-sixties, describes Weidlinger as "a real collaborator," something the decisive Bunshaft had never needed before.

Bunshaft's ability to master this shift in style—not just architectural style, but style of production allowed him to maintain his position of authority at SOM. He had

changed with the times. Almost instantaneous success at the Emhart Corporation, Bloomfield, Connecticut (1963) and the Beinecke Library, New Haven (1963) proved that Bunshaft had more than one gear. He was not SOM's chief designer any longer and never again commanded its vernacular, but he could still act with authority. He could parcel out his resources. When, in 1963, the San Francisco office wanted to work with Davis Allen on the interiors of the Mauna Kea Resort (1965), they sought advice from William S. Brown, the head of SOM's office in New York. On his approval, they then asked permission of Gordon Bunshaft to approach Davis Allen about working on the project.[18] Allen then brought to Mauna Kea some of the aesthetic he had managed to insert (with Bunshaft) into the Chase Manhattan Bank (1961), so that if it wasn't Bunshaft, it wasn't not Bunshaft either. Indeed the ubiquity of Davis Allen became another manifestation of Bunshaft's taste and style.[19] After reading an article on interiors designed by the Chicago office in *Interiors* one has some doubts as to whether, as claimed in the article, there was a distinctive "Chicago" style of interior design.[20]

Yet it is important not to characterize Bunshaft too broadly. The stereotypical Bunshaft is just a little too easy to grasp: the decisive man in the corner office, the man who convinced with conviction, who could be hard on his colleagues. Once he sent Natalie de Blois home to change her clothes (he did not like the color green—didn't everyone know that SOM didn't use green?); he turned his back on anyone he wished not to speak with—whether a partner or a partner's wife.[21] Even his tone toward his own wife, Nina, could sometimes leave those within earshot feeling compassion for her. How could she put up with that treatment? But it was not kick down and kiss up—his bluntness was equal opportunity. Bunshaft was not afraid to speak truth to power, as his letter to Lyndon Johnson about one of the exhibitions at Johnson's Presidential Library reveals: "The only sour note in your Library, it seems to me, is the Political Campaign Exhibit. The subject is a fine one but the exhibit seems to have been done without the slightest sense of design or regard for the space or walls …. It all looks like a poor trade show." Johnson's reply was gracious.[22]

Bunshaft could spot talent; he would draw people into his circle and reward them. After Roger Radford undertook the programming of a commission in Bunshaft's absence, he was pulled aside by the great man: " I was leaving the office to go to lunch, and he was with me then and he said, "Where are you going to lunch?" And I said, "I don't know." He said, "Well, let's go over here." So we went to some sandwich shop, and we talked a little …."[23] Bunshaft asked about his background, his training, and his interests in architecture. "And in the discussions that we had," goes on Radford, "it was always a give and take. And continued to be, throughout the following years, you know." Although, he admitted, "[s]ometimes it was more give than take, and sometimes …."[24] Others report the same experience: when Bunshaft saw something he liked, the door opened.

In preparing designs for the National Commercial Bank, Jeddah, the senior designer on the project Tom Killian (SOM 1963–90) reports that Bunshaft took an initial dislike to him. ("You're the guy that does triangles.") Later Bunshaft saw Killian's proposal for stacked "V's" and liked what he saw and pulled him into the project. Later still, as the project approached completion, Killian's partner, the architect Françoise Bollack, saw the design and commented that the reveal for the ventilation register, that served visually as a kind of molding, was inappropriately cut in at the corners. Bunshaft agreed and the completed building is without them. Nonetheless, he could reach out even when his own interests were not being directly served. In 1971, Linda Flannery, a disgruntled employee leaving SOM, wrote a long letter to Bunshaft lamenting the firm's lack of support for design and criticizing the business-minded mentality of the newer partners. "Mr. Bunshaft," she wrote, "you are the only partner who is respected, without exception by everyone in the this firm." She appealed to him to revitalize the firm. "I'm sure you must care about the firm and its future and that underneath all your gruffness have a true concern for your employees …." What Bunshaft said to her, or indeed if he spoke to her at all, is not known, but penciled on the letter are phone numbers. Bunshaft clearly tried to call her—and thought the letter worth preserving.[25] Was he telling us something about himself? Or did Bunshaft want his correspondent to say what he could not say openly about his colleagues?

The Silent Bunshaft

One aspect of Bunshaft's work still needs to be assessed. What does it say about him that he was so close to a number of prominent artists and sculptors? Was he a different person with them? He certainly wasn't a pushover. Despite all the talk about a "team approach," Bunshaft ordered Natalie de Blois to redesign the northeast court at Connecticut General after he was dissatisfied with Isamu Noguchi's proposal.[26] Noguchi was not always happy in a collaboration with Bunshaft. "One-sided" was Noguchi's phrase for it where "collaboration" meant bending to the architect's will. Nonetheless, he brought a different tone to his relationships with artists. The extensive correspondence with Jean Dubuffet and Henry Moore, for example, is both playful and witty, describing cheerful conversations, and looking forward to further jovial meetings. Typical is this cover letter (July

National Commercial Bank, Jeddah, Saudi Arabia, elevation, 1978. Felt-tipped pen and color pencil on tracing paper, 55 ½ x 30 ¼" inches

Chase Manhattan Bank, New York, New York

one extra-architectural pleasure he allowed himself: "I don't like the word 'collector.' That's too fancy, but it's a kind of a disease. First you buy one or two things, and then you buy more and more, and stud it wherever you can." It was also the one area in which Bunshaft could match his interests to those of the firm.[29] He might never be the country-club architect in tweeds, but service as trustee at the Museum of Modern Art brought him into contact with progressive businessmen and he allowed his artistic interests to be part of his public image.[30] Bunshaft relished the process of selecting the works of art to be put in the offices at Chase Manhattan and remained good friends with Seymour Knox II (1898–1990), chairman of Marine Midland Bank, in Buffalo, with whom he shared a passion for contemporary art. Knox donated a major addition (designed by Bunshaft) to the Albright Art (later Albright-Knox) Gallery in Buffalo.

Bunshaft's correspondence with his artist-friends makes it seem as if they are all speaking the same language and maybe, in a sense, they were. Bunshaft believed that his buildings had to speak for themselves. Better yet, as he told the *New York Times* in 1972: "I like my architecture to speak for itself. Well, anyhow, to speak for me."[31] In describing the Albright addition, he commented to the *Buffalo Evening News* in 1962: "The building speaks for itself."[32] In his long interviews with Arthur Drexler, Reinhold Martin notes, he "scarcely acknowledges the intersection of architecture with analytic discourse."[33] A decade later, as he wrote to Owen Luder declining an invitation to deliver the first RIBA Westbourne Lecture: "I don't like to ~~give talks~~ talk to large groups so I haven't for the past ~~20-30~~ forty years. I also believe that the buildings I have designed should speak for me."[34] But perhaps it was that silence that he shared with artists? His friend Jean Dubuffet thought writing about art was inevitably cold: "Written language seems to me a bad instrument. As an instrument of expression, it seems to deliver only a dead remnant of thought, more or less as clinkers from the fire."[35] In fact, Henry Moore had his own misgivings about delivering opinions about works of sculpture observing that, "For a sculptor or a painter to speak or write, in public, about his job, very often is a mistake. It (perhaps) releases (some of the) urge & tension needed to do his work with intensity–."[36] In the company of artists unwilling to explain their art, it

31, 1972) to Moore sending on a review of David Mitchinson's *Henry Moore Unpublished Drawings* (1972) from the *New York Times*. "I hope you will like the review. It seems to be very thoughtful and affectionate one, it is hard to visualize Mr. John Canaday being affectionate as he is quite a sour puss as a rule."[27] The correspondence with both Moore and Dubuffet, though it often deals with matters of business, could be tender. To Dubuffet he wrote (November 3, 1972), after the installation of his *Group of Three Trees* in front of Chase Manhattan: "I enjoyed your visit here tremendously. I felt that although I have known you, off and on, for many years, this is the first time we really became closer." And to Dubuffet Bunshaft, wrote enthusiastically (November 22, 1972): "It gave us a tremendous feeling of warmth and closeness to you."[28] Were these just client-client relations? Was Bunshaft just anxious to curry the favor of those he needed to complete his architectural works; the artists keen to get on with a client whose investment mattered to them? Perhaps.. Though he was at pains not to call himself a collector, his dedication to art seems to have been the

Pan American Life Insurance Company, New Orleans, Louisiana

Smith College dormitory, Northampton, Massachusetts

Libbey-Owens-Ford Glass, Toledo, Ohio

was as if they justified Bunshaft's own uncertain silences. Perhaps only in the context of SOM—a large firm with spokesmen and press releases, and able project managers, could it be sustained.

Bunshaft's frequent indifference to the firm was painful to many of his fellow partners of whose talents he could be dismissive ("Owings was a brilliant salesman").[37] He never successfully mentored a young designer or brought a designer of comparable skills to the partnership: the office was there for his convenience, and after he went they'd just have to manage. The Chicago offices thrived as Graham, Netsch, Goldsmith and Khan matured under William Hartmann. Bunshaft initially tried to discourage Chuck Bassett, who developed independently on the West Coast, supported by Owings. In Washington, Owings helped advance David Childs. Today the "children" of Bassett, Netsch, and Childs run SOM. Only late in life did Bunshaft seem to embrace the idea of SOM as a team. On viewing the film prepared for the fiftieth anniversary of SOM he delivered a brief speech recalling his beginnings with the firm and critiquing the film for its focus on half a dozen individuals. "The truth of the matter," he said, "is that we're all very ordinary people. If we'd been on our own, we'd be nothing. The fact that we're a team … has given all of us, to different degrees, opportunities to go beyond what could have been done if we hadn't been part of this group …. I don't think there are many people who come into this world who could be Corbusier or Mies or even Wright. I don't think we've done a proper job in crediting all you people. That's it."[38]

In the end Bunshaft remains a mystery, yet we do have a better grasp on what he contributed to SOM. It was not just fine buildings, although there were many of them. It was not just his characteristic style of operation, although that is what people often see first. Even though he did not articulate these issues eloquently, Bunshaft believed that serious issues were at play in the entire design process: human needs, aspirations, dreams.[39] He also believed that architectural issues needed to be resolved swiftly because money and time were at stake (and because he could work quickly) and he balanced that belief by striving for the highest possible artistic quality in whatever came under his hand. Finally, Bunshaft's genuine passion for art, his belief that he, too, was an artist, guaranteed to others that he had these higher values at his core. SOM will never have another Bunshaft—times have changed—but the qualities of conviction and adaptability, of integrity and excellence are still essential for the partnership.

Acknowledgements: I am grateful for conversations about Gordon Bunshaft with David Childs, Tom Killian, Carol Krinsky, Leon Moed, and Jennifer Radford. Thanks also to Janet Parks for making materials available from the Bunshaft Architectural Drawings and Papers at Avery Library, Columbia University. Kyle Toth at Vassar College provided helpful assistance. Roger Duffy's and Peter MacKeith's questions provoked the issues raised in this article.

1 From a letter written by David Bunshaft, September 18, 1945, to his son Gordon, on meeting the family of his future daughter-in-law. Gordon Bunshaft, Architectural Drawings and Papers, Avery Architectural & Fine Arts Library, Department of Drawings & Archives, Columbia University, Correspondence, Series 1:6. (Cited hereafter as Bunshaft, Architectural Drawings and Papers, Avery Library.)

2 "When he decided that an idea was good he did not deviate from it, having always made firm decisions—to become an architect, to attend MIT, to attach himself to SOM's small practice, to recognize a good solution and keep to it rather than rethink problems endlessly." Carol Krinsky, Gordon Bunshaft of Skidmore, Owings & Merrill (Cambridge and New York, 1988), p. 332.

3 See, for example, the letter of James Babb to Whitney Griswold concerning Beinecke Library, August 10, 1959, Yale University Archives, RU 22 YRG 2-A, 1963-A-002, Box 141, folder 1285.

4 For example, see the discussion of Bunshaft's role in denying membership in the American Academy of Arts and Letters to Robert Venturi, David Jacobs, "The Establishment's architect-plus," New York Times, July 23, 1972, pp. 20–21. Or in blocking Venturi's design for the Transportation Square Office Building, Washington (1967). See also Vincent Scully on Venturi (originally published, 1989) in Modern Architecture and Other Essays (Princeton, 2003), pp. 277–78.

5 "The Architects from Skid's Row," Fortune 57 (January 1958), pp. 137–40; 210, 212, 215.

6 William H. Whyte Jr., The Organization Man (New York, 1956), p. 7. See "$2-Billion worth of Design by Conference," Business Week, December 4, 1954, pp. 96–102.

7 "Skidmore, Owings & Merrill architects, U.S.A.," (Fall 1950), p. 5.

8 "Designers for a Busy World: Mood for Working," Newsweek (May 4, 1959), pp. 97–100. The quotations are from p. 97 and p. 100.

9 John Winter, Adrian Forty, and Thomas Weaver, "John Winter in conversation with Adrian Forty &Thomas Weaver," AA Files 63 (2011), p. 23.

10 Roger Radford, Oral History of Roger Nicholas Radford, interviewed by Sharon Zane (Chicago: Art Institute, 2008), p. 141. See also David Jacobs, "The Establishment's architect-plus," p. 16: "This meant [referring to the period of the nineteen-fifties] that he designed or supervised everything that came out of the office...."

11 Bunshaft was quite specific about the buildings over which he had control, see Krinsky, Gordon Bunshaft, pp. 335–38. Here is a preliminary list of Bunshaft-influenced buildings up to 1962: Fiberglas Building, New York (1948, destroyed); Pan-American Life, New Orleans (1951); Grout Park School, Schenectady, NY (1954); Harry A. Conte School, New Haven, CT (1955); Smith College Dormitories (Cutter Ziskind House), Northampton, MA (1956); CIBA/Geigy, Ardsley, NY (1956); Research Office, Wyeth Laboratories, Radnor, PA (1957); Ford Foundation, New York (1957, destroyed); Girl Scouts of America, New York (1957); the Medical Towers Building, Houston, Texas (1957); International Arrivals Building, Idlewild/JFK (1958); CBS Laboratory and Technical Center, Stamford, CT (1958); General Mills Headquarters, Golden Valley, Minnesota (1958); Chapel and Meditation House, Colgate University (1959); Banco di Bogotá, Colombia (1960); Libbey-Owens-Ford Glass, Toledo, Ohio (1960); Noxell-Noxema, Warehouses and Headquarters, Cockeysville, MD (from 1960); Seatrain Lines, New York (1960); Union Carbide, Westchester County (1960); Equitable Building (1961); Short Hills Mall, Short Hills. NJ (1962); CIL (Telus Tower), Montreal, PQ (1962).

12 "Bunshaft is a vital cog in the machine, serving as partner in charge of design for most jobs originating in New York. He is often called to other offices for consultation." "$2-Billion worth of Design...." Business Week 1954, p. 103 (see note 6). As Fortune noted: "And his influence on design is sometimes felt far from the New York office." Fortune 1958, p. 215 (see note 5).

13 "SOM's Details of Distinction," Architectural Forum 112 (June 1960), pp. 124–29; quotation from p. 124.

14 Allan Temko, "American Architecture: Down to Skin and Bones," Journal of the American Institute of Architects, n. 30/5 (November 1958), pp. 19–23.

15 "For architect's only," Architectural Forum 100 (April 1954), p. 172.

16 See Fortune 1958, p. 215.

17 Krinsky 1988, p. 138 (see note 2).

18 See SOM Archives (San Francisco), Job 137, Box 1722, "Interoffice Communication #2," letters from John Weese to William S. Brown, October 25, 1963; to Gordon Bunshaft, November 1, 1963; undated letter from John Weese to Davis Allen (later in November).

19 See Maeve Slavin, Davis Allen: Forty Years of Interior Design at Skidmore, Owings & Merrill (New York, 1990).

20 J. A., "SOM: The Chicago Office of Skidmore, Owings & Merrill," Interiors (January 1959), pp., 90–109.

21 For clients, like Frazar Wilde, the conviction could be managed. For example, in developing the plans for Connecticut General, Roger Radford reports: "The owner wanted alternative solutions. And we did, I think, six solutions, but only one was Gordon interested in. And the others—you know, the meeting would start, and we'd rush through the other five, and then would concentrate on the one." Roger Radford, Oral History of Roger Nicholas Radford, p. 44. In social situations, however, Bunshaft's convictions often came across to people as rude.

22 Letter from Gordon Bunshaft to Lyndon B. Johnson, June 1, 1971, Bunshaft, Architectural Drawings and Papers, Avery Library, Correspondence, Series 1:4.

23 Oral History of Roger Nicholas Radford, p. 35

24 Ibid., p. 37

25 Bunshaft, Architectural Drawings and Papers, Avery Library, Correspondence, Series 1:12.

26 See "The team approach: a round-table discussion of how Connecticut General got just what it wanted from designers," Architectural Design 5 (1958), p. 57." Author's interview with Natalie de Blois, 17 February 2005.

27 Bunshaft, Architectural Drawings and Papers, Avery Library, Correspondence, Series 1:4.

28 Bunshaft, Architectural Drawings and Papers, Avery Library, Correspondence, Series 1:9.

29 "Bunshaft and Noguchi," Bunshaft grew up with the words of someone like Royal Barry Willis in his ear: "Disinterested civic service is every architect's duty," he wrote in recommending joining the local art commission. Royal Barry Wills, *This Business of Architecture* (New York, 1941), p. 63.

30 As he told Betty Blum: "One of the reasons I thought I'd be a designer and stay with that firm was I had the feeling in those times, the early nineteen-thirties, that architecture was a gentleman's profession and that they were all club members and they got work at clubs. And it was a great deal like that. I figured the way I am and being Jewish and stuff—although that didn't enter into it—that I wasn't geared for getting jobs." *Oral History of Gordon Bunshaft*, interviewed by Betty J. Blum (Chicago, 1990; revised edition, 2000), p. 230. He repeated these comments to David Jacobs, "The Establishment's architect-plus," *New York Times*, July 23, 1972, p. 16.

31 Jacobs, "The Establishment's architect-plus," p. 12.

32 "Addition to Gallery 'Speaks for Itself,' Architect Says," *Buffalo Evening News*, January 20, 1962.

33 See Reinhold Martin, "The Bunshaft Tapes: A Preliminary Report," *Journal of Architectural Education* 54 (November 2000), p. 81.

34 Bunshaft, Architectural Drawings and Papers, Avery Library, Correspondence, Series 1:5, undated.

35 "Anticultural Positions," from a lecture given by Dubuffet at the Arts Club of Chicago, December 20, 1951, reproduced in *Theories and Documents of Contemporary Art: a Sourcebook of Artists' Writings*, ed. Kristine Stiles and Peter Howard Selz (Berkeley, 2012), p. 195.

36 The quotation came from an article in *The Listener* (1937) and was reproduced in books on Moore in 1944 and 1966. See *Henry Moore: Writings and Conversations*, ed. Allan G. Wilkinson (Berkeley, 2002), p. 20.

37 *Oral History of Gordon Bunshaft*, p. 49.

38 The transcription of his remarks was by Hill Burgess and sent to Raul de Armas and Jane Moos, November 11, 1986. Bunshaft, Architectural Drawings and Papers, Avery Library, Correspondence, Series 1:5.

39 For example, one cannot imagine that he read Owings' frivolous description of a revived lower Manhattan as theme park in *The Spaces in Between: An Architect's Journey* (Boston, 1973), p. 164 with any pleasure.

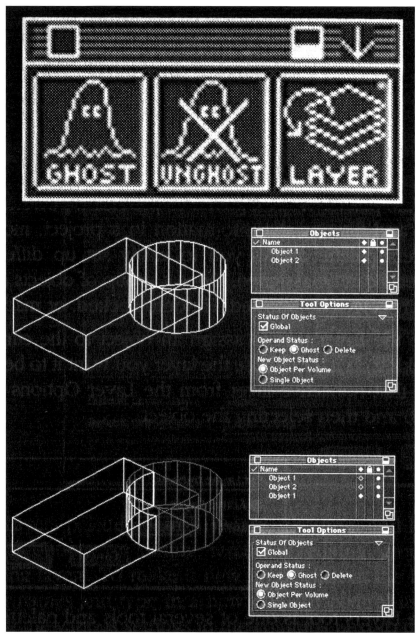

Detail of interface design, Form Z, ghosting and layering commands

Clear all Ghosted

Thomas de Monchaux

Interviewer: "You've done some flying, haven't you?"
Frank Gehry: "I sit in the cockpit sometimes. I do know how to do it, a little bit."
—*Conversations with Frank Gehry*, 2003[1]

In contemporary architectural practice, the condition of authorship—of determinate agency between the desires and designs of any given individual and subsequent built work—has been destabilized by three factors. The first is nothing new. The second dates to a very particular time and place. The third is big and getting bigger and, haunting the others, is precipitating a long dilemma in what we mean when we say a design has been designed, or a drawing drawn.

The first factor is the social and operational organization of architectural firms, in which design work—historically always a matter of intense collaboration between specialists and generalists, thinkers and makers, tacticians and technicians, even between patrons and architects—enters the world under the brand of a founding architect, often one whose personal presence in that collaboration has long since receded. This is nothing new; the design and construction of buildings has always been a vast conspiracy disguised as a singular event. All buildings are, to varying degrees, ghostwritten.

Architects, lacking the material or social capital of the patrons whose money they spend and whose retinue they enhance, benefit from perpetuating the Wright/ Roark myth of the lonely and contrarian genius. The myth provides glamour, and even a touch of the tragic, which can translate, meeting after meeting, into real power. But—even reinforced by its small participation in today's vast star-systems of mediagenic images and contemporary celebrity culture—this myth is paper-thin. And it's getting thinner: requiring a slow accumulation of necessarily diverse knowledge and client networks, architectural practice has long been a game for old men (almost always men). However, with fifty the new forty and eighty the new seventy, the old men are getting older, and the support systems invested in their never retiring ever more elaborate—radically reducing, the status and signification of "late work." This may be especially the case in the contemporary "high tech" mode of design, a mode whose systematized and standardized components at first seemed to offer a respite from any individual designer's signature style, but have now become acutely the medium for just that—each partnership or workshop generating its parallel mechanical and structural defaults and devices, propagating systems of ever more seeming universality, but ever more actual irreconcilability. Mannerist individuation has become, in this case perhaps, a measure of the anxiety of influence.

The second factor dates to 1985, the year when (by his own account in the "Introduction" to the book *Chora L Works*, documenting their subsequent collaboration), architect Bernard Tschumi "thought I would introduce Peter Eisenman to [Jacques] Derrida, and invite them to work together on one of La Villette's gardens."[2] The invitation was itself an expression of authorial indeterminacy: in winning the design of Paris's La Villette park, Tschumi's authorial role in its subsequent fifteen-year development was somewhere between designer and curator, architect and master-planner. Along with Tschumi's notable grid-point array of boxy red *folies* (and layered above and below them those graphically-calligraphic pathways suggesting cinematic pans and cuts in one's experience of them), the architect distributed portions of the park to designers such as John Hejduk and Eisenman (whose work remains unbuilt), and artists like Claes Oldenburg (who would eventually produce a landscape installation).

The epistolary encounter that resulted between Eisenman and Derrida, between architect and philosopher, is its own well-worn subject. Within a consideration of the idea of authorship in architecture, the meeting is of interest because it represents an encounter between a designer whose own documented design process and self-description has long resisted confessions of willfulness, impulse, or otherwise visibly decisive desire; and a thinker whose discourse introduced, among much else,

Cartoon, *Manchester Evening News*, May 10, 1957, as illustrated in *The Architecture Machine*, Nicholas Negroponte, 1970

a critical indeterminacy between the status or truth of a word or deed as intended by its speaker/writer/actor, and that same event as received by its perceiver, or as situated within a mediating system of grammar and syntax, or any such structural armature.

This sort of post-structuralist thinking has as one of its origins the 1968 observation by Roland Barthes that, "writing is that destruction of every voice, of every point of origin. Writing is that neutral, composite, oblique space where our subject slips away … starting with the very identity of the body writing. … As soon as a fact is narrated no longer with a view to acting directly on reality… that is to say, finally outside of any function other than that of the practice [of narration] itself, this disconnection occurs, the voice loses its origin, the author enters into his own death, writing begins."[3] The philosophical deconstruction associated with Derrida is one means of addressing that destruction and disconnection, in which a written text achieves a contingent "truth" independent of its writer, and dependent on its reader.

For writing in relation to speech, one can substitute drawing (especially architectural drafting) in relation to the built environment. Eisenman's most direct expression on the matter is perhaps his 1987 essay "Misread-

ing," which addresses his own early house designs. In those designs, elaborately serial rules-based operations on an increasingly-transformed prismatic volume and baseline grid—usually angular rotations and linear shifts, and the use of those displacements to enact additive or subtractive events known to subsequent software-users as Boolean operations—produced draftsmanly artifacts that bore an indeterminate relationship to the idea of a house as conventionally conceived of as a geometrical and material accommodation of program and site. Although these designs were articulated within axonometric and isometric conventions relating two-dimensional notation to three-dimensional space, the "houses" also deliberately destabilized conventional spatial readings. "The current work is perhaps best conceived as a series of palimpsests," wrote Eisenman, "a dynamic locus of figures and partially-obscured traces. Site-specific and scale non-specific, they record and respond to change. Although they are directed, they are ultimately authorless."[4]

"That is," Eisenman clarified, "they refuse any single authoritative reading. Their 'truth' is constantly in flux." Such an attitude, which accommodates continuous fluctuations in the verity or "truthiness" of any given reading, which accommodates a massively parallel pursuit down iteratively branching yes-no interrogations and evaluations of successive possibilities, might be one way of describing the default setting of what Nicholas Negroponte (writing, like Roland Barthes, in 1968), described as "the architecture machine." Dismissing the mere automation of existing analog procedures, and the converse adaption of those procedures to mechanical optimums, Negroponte emphasized "a third way in which machines can assist the design process: [that process] considered as evolutionary, can be presented to a machine, also considered as evolutionary, and a mutual training, resilience, and growth can be developed."[5]

Negroponte located the critical creative or destructive event not in information as initially or ultimately inputted or outputted by machine or architect, but in the system of mutual training and expressive exchange itself, directed yet authorless, that developed between them: "Each should track the other's design maneuvers, evoking a rhetoric that cannot be anticipated." And, as Negroponte quoted software engineers Warren Brodey and Nilo

Lindgren, "What was mere noise and disorder or distraction before, becomes pattern and sense; information has been metabolized out of noise."[6]

With these assertions, we arrive at the presence of computing and the history of mechanical and digital computation in architecture, the third factor in the contemporary destabilization of architectural authorship. For a long time, architectural historiography on this subject mostly concerned itself with an opposition between "the computer" and "the hand" as a way of drawing and communicating. Lately, the history writing has been more about distinguishing between computation as an analytic tool for optimizing structural or other operational performance through the iterative testing of parametrically-variable models, and computation as a more directly creative endeavor by architects. Developing this historiography requires new modes of oral history and recollection-collection, largely because its events don't leave the familiar historiographical traces of stable documents and static artifacts. A prototype for this practice is the exhibition series *Archeology of the Digital* (inaugurated at the Canadian Center for Architecture in the summer of 2013 and curated by architect Greg Lynn), a curatorial project that compiles major works at the late-analog/early-digital, late nineteen-eighties/early nineties, moment in architecture. These works include major unbuilt designs by Peter Eisenman and his contemporary Frank Gehry, along with their associated documentary ephemera and accounts. Lynn's own early independent work, especially as collected in his 1999 monograph *Animate Form*, catalyzed a moment in architectural research and software use in which, as Lynn put it at the time, "the forms of a dynamically conceived architecture may be shaped in association with virtual motion and force," as modeled in software.[7]

Deploying something of Lynn's own historiographical method for digital archeology, I gave him a call.[8] I asked him about computers and their effect on the other two factors that destabilize the idea of authorship in architecture: the distributed and corporate creativity of the atelier, and the self-conscious authorlessness asserted for the works of Deconstruction-deploying architects like Peter Eisenman.

On the first factor, Lynn observed, "One of the obstacles to creative integration of computational technology into

"Drawing on the IBM Cambridge Scientific Center's 2250, plotted on a Calcomp plotter," as reproduced in *The Architecture Machine*, Nicholas Negroponte, 1970

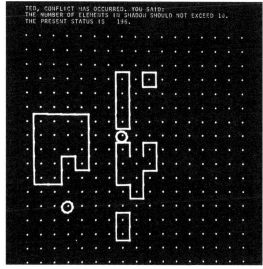

Screen capture, URBAN5 computer-aided design prototype, as illustrated in *The Architecture Machine*, Nicholas Negroponte, 1970

corporate culture is that it set up this whole realm of negotiation, a confusion of hierarchy between the CAD operator and the senior designer. The late nineties saw a huge confusion in offices around the role of the computer." Looking over the shoulder of the CAD operator, Lynn recalls, a designer would ask for a particular operation or modification to a digital model, and the operator would explain that, in fact, no, the software couldn't do it. "The intern would never say, you can't do this with cardboard," reflected Lynn, "but at that moment there was this assumption that every design action had its exact software corollary. I used to describe it as "file-conversion-as-design-method": take it out of one software into another so you could slice it, out of that software into another so you could unfold it, then take it into another …" The assumption of the possibility of one-to-one mapping between design intention and computational action generated an interference—what Negroponte might call noise—not between architect and machine, but within the social hierarchies of the architectural office itself.

Frank Gehry has described the experience of the designer looking over the operator's shoulder at the computer screen in this way: "When I'm looking at a computer image of one of my buildings, when I'm working with it, I have to keep an ideal 'dream' in my head. I have an idea for a building and it's visually clear in my head, but I have to hold on to its image while looking at some terrible image on a screen. That requires too much energy and concentration for me, and I can only do it for a few minutes at a time. Then I have to run out of the room screaming."[9] One effect of the anecdote is to assert a primacy for the formal dream in the architect's head over the terrible computational artifact that is its inadequate representation.

In the practice of Peter Eisenman, a pursuit of the converse—situating the dream into the proximate intelligence of software and the rendering of its image into human hands—may have been the case. In 1987, Lynn was working on drawings of Eisenman's unbuilt but epochal Biocentrum building for the University of Frankfurt. The project consisted of five parallel bar buildings housing laboratories, arrayed and aligned much like a sample of five successive transformations in Eisenman's earlier house drawings, linked by a circulation and social spine whose encounter with those bars notionally

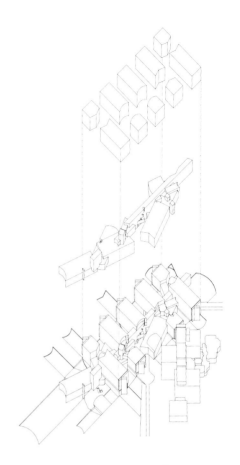

Exploded axonometric, Biocentrum project by Peter Eisenman, as illustrated in *Deconstructivist Architecture*, exhibition catalogue, 1988

induced complex volumetric operations, generally Boolean, upon them. As described in the catalog of the 1988 Museum of Modern Art *Deconstructivist Architecture* exhibit, in which it was a centerpiece, in the Biocentrum, "sometimes one form passes over or under another; sometimes one form is simply embedded within another; sometimes one form eats into another; sometimes both forms are disturbed and a new form is produced. The project becomes a complex exchange between solid, void, and transparency."[10]

Lynn's recollection of the project is telling: "Peter had been chasing the perfect procedural process for a long time, looking for this perfect ability to rewind a project backward and forward or within itself. And with the

Biocentrum it was really there." Lynn remembers the authorial process that produced this perfect method as a complex exchange between conventional and computational tools, mediated by the long-distance communication methods of the day: phone, fax, and FedEx. "There was this hope that the computer was going to set the plan geometry," he notes, "but it hadn't been going that well. I just sat there drafting what the supercomputer was doing at Ohio State [the university where Chris Yessios, a pioneer of CAD and a designer of the influential early 3D-modelling software Form*Z, was co-teaching with Eisenman an early computational design studio called the Fractal Studio], "and we'd get these Fed Exes from them in the morning of that day's stack of 8 ½ x 11-inch printouts and assemble them and mark them up—on iteration 117 replace figure A with figure C, for instance—and then we'd fax it back in strips. I was sitting there listening to all of this, trying to get the updated plan done with the adjustable triangle, working against the machine like John Henry, before the next Fed Ex would arrive."

Is it coincidence or convergence that these three primary figures of the notional Deconstructivist moment in architectural history—Eisenman, Tschumi, and Gehry—were also the earliest and most influential adopters of digital design methods and other architecture machines?

The simplest explanation is that the complex surficial and volumetric geometries that interested these designers required, and therefore drove, the development of new representational tools. Gehry's office was famously an early user of the CATIA surface-modeling software developed for aerospace use by Dessault Systemes. Eisenman's office was similarly in consultation with Chris Yessios' Form*Z, and Tschumi's deployment of an early incarnation of the same software in his own 1994 "paperless studio" at Columbia University also influenced that software's development. "Since we discovered the CATIA software program," Gehry asserts in *Gehry Talks*, "they've been working on making the system fit our way of working. So they now have a new enhanced CATIA that they're going to install here, which … allows us to control the architectural process to within seven decimal points of accuracy. That's what I like about it."[11]

But perhaps there is more to it than mere accuracy. "Peter thinks like a computer," Greg Lynn observed, "and

Frank draws like a computer." To those assertions one might add that Bernard sees like a computer.

To *think* like a computer, as in the house drawings and the Biocentrum project, is to dream of perfect procedure, of an infinitely extending seriality of which the drawn and built structure is a kind of extracted sample. To *draw* like a computer is something different but adjacent: a graphic tendency towards wireframes or towards the periodical or informational transformations of a single unbroken line—towards the generation, as Negroponte put it, of pattern and sense out of a base condition of distraction and disorder: in effect, to make noise in order to notice a signal within it. Such a mode of drawing has been compellingly described by Horst Bredekamp in this way: "The courses of Gehry's lines, which come together into an overall form seemingly against their will, offer a cosmos of related webs. … He controls the course of his […] motor activity as if from the perspective of an observer.… Therein lies what is perhaps [his drawings'] most important calling: not to obey their creator but to astonish him."[12] "How long does it take you to do a sketch?" an interviewer once asked Gehry. "Fifteen seconds," he answered, like a computer, "… but I do a lot of them."[13]

This looking-to-be-astonished gaze at one's own act of drawing may be, again, different but adjacent to the techniques of collage, layering, and palimpsest with which Bernard Tschumi sees like a computer: a way of seeing that distinguishes critically between setting and event, background pattern and foreground event, that establishes an economy of notionally updated and superimposed frames in which only the variable becomes visible. "When Tschumi did the paperless studio," Lynn recalled, "a week into it, he grabbed me and said, "it's incredible, the computer worked by layers." This was right after the design of the park at La Villette, the influential drawings of which emphasized the layered superimposition of geometrical systems, movement patterns, and existing site conditions.

Tschumi would later express a kind of simultaneous avowal and disavowal of the layering technique: "The palimpsest device had been important to my work since I used it in the [*Manhattan*] *Transcripts*. [I]n the early nineteen-eighties, history was viewed by academics as a series of layers; many architects [like] Also Rossi claimed that architecture always related to the circumstances of the past. [Another] precedent was the fade-in/fade-out notion derived from film, which I had used [before La Villette]. These … notions were fascinating, but at the same time enormously restricting in that used together they produced an inherently formal operation. The images that resulted would be fixed images as opposed to abstract strategies, so even though the palimpsest might have been an interesting path, it couldn't be followed."[14]

A cycle of avowal and disavowal about the creative process behind any given project is itself, perhaps, part of the act of authorship, especially given how any project authors—by privately changing and publicly identifying—its creator, as much as the creator authors a project. The authorlessness in which these architects may be particularly interested has a quality of inevitability—an update of the old Modernist dream of a seamless translation of functional operations into formal conditions without the interference of style or desire or anxiety of influence. "There's the computer as alibi," said Lynn, "this thing of 'if I can get the computer to get me there where I want to go, through analytic means, then I'll be unassailable.'"

This particular use of the computer may have its own archaeology in the operational dream of what Lynn called "the cult of the base drawing." "When I came up in the mid-'eighties," he remembered, "we came up through this base drawing, which really came out of Xerox technology, the ability to enlarge and reduce and replicate with photocopies." The base drawing would be a record of site conditions and resized and superimposed details—"site-specific and scale non-specific," as Eisenman would later describe his house drawings—that, copied and recopied, and while seemingly being only an

ever-better record of existing conditions, would actually seamlessly come to be a record of future conditions: a system of marks delineating the design. "There was this moment," remembered Lynn, "of seeing who could produce the most fertile base drawings: all the layering and then the other thing of editing and extruding from that—a method that the computer really played into."

Of course, to trace perfectly is to eliminate any trace at all of the layers below the active layer. Authorship as a concept may be valuable to architects to the extent that it reinforces or undermines this condition of inevitability: this condition of contingency so absolute that it is no contingency at all, but a kind of immediacy—a perfect simultaneous translation between site logic and design logic, rather than an imposition of the latter on the former. To use the word *author* in reference to any creative process or project, but perhaps especially in reference to design—which is to say *drawing*—is to especially evoke that other calligraphic act, *writing*. The notional capacity of writing to detach itself from both the embodied event of its inscription and from any fixed content it has the capacity to convey—from what made it, and from what it may make—may capture most precisely the interest of architects in search of this quality of inevitability.

One way of describing the coincidence of pioneering computational tools in architecture with the use of philosophical Deconstruction in architecture is to notice that both were methods of generating ghosts. In his book, *Derrida's Haunt*, written about Deconstruction in philosophy and the modes of architecture he would assemble in the 1988 MoMA exhibit on the subject, Mark Wigley quotes Jacques Derrida's elliptical observation that,

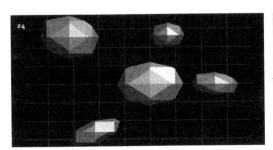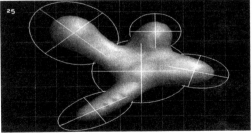

"Disconnected primitives used to compose an isomorphic polysurface" and "Isomorphic polysurface with primitives fused into a single surface," as illustrated in *Animate Form*, Greg Lynn, 1999.

HOUSE IV.

TRANSFORMATIONS (FORMAL OPERATIONS)

A_1

BASE CONDITION OF VOLUME. WHILE UNEQUAL DIMENSIONALITY IN HORIZONTAL AND VERTICAL DIMENSIONS THERE ARE
X_1 Neutral ~~cube~~; no internal ~~n~~or external influences. THE INTENTION TO ENGENDER SPATIAL OPPOSITIONS IN OBJECT THROUGH A SEQUENCE OF TRANSFORMATIONS BEGINS.
THIS FIRST ~~SET~~ SET OF TRANSFORMATIONS CONCERNED WITH ARTICULATION OF CENTER AND EDGE; EDGE AND SIDE GRAIN; SYMMETRY AND ASYMMETRY, IS SO AS TO CHARGE THE ORIGINAL NEUTRAL CUBE WITH A STRUCTURE OF FORMAL RELATIONSHIPS

X_2 Center square cut out; distinguishes ~~center and edge surface.~~ Size~~—~~
VOLUME (VOID) AND AN EDGE PLANE (SURFACE)
size of cut out distinguishes center and volume. No distinction between
VOID (F)   surround (a)
exterior surfaces (A) Bi-axial and bi-lateral symmetry.

A_2

— THIS SLOT
X_3 Center square cut out, extended to create a vertical ~~slot~~ Distinguishes
SLOT
2 "A" sides and 2 "B" sides. ~~This distinction is literal and unambiguous.~~
AND SECTION IS   DISTINGUISHING
Plan now ~~is~~ a series of layers with a ~~distinction in direction,~~ distinguishing
a lateral and orthogonal axis. THERE IS NOW A SIDE GRAIN ON SIDE A
AND AN END GRAIN ON SIDE B. TWO OF THE THREE ~~PROGRAMMATIC SPATIAL~~ OPPOSITIONS
ARE NOW IN OPERATION ALBEIT IN A LITERAL AND UNAMBIGUOUS MANNER I.E. THAT
~~IS WITH NO POTENTIAL VIRTUALLY~~ VIRTUAL CAPACITY.
OPPOSITE OR REVERSE
X_{3a} ~~Alternative~~ extension of a center square cut out along an horizontal axis.
In this condition all sides (vertical surfaces) are equal. ~~Plan remains~~
EQUAL
~~the same.~~ Volume reads as a series of horizontal slabs with a dominant
horizontal axis. NO LAYERING IN PLAN OR SECTION.

A_{3b}
A CONDITION ~~SIMILAR TO THE BASE~~ CONDITION
X_{3b} Superimposition of X_3 and X_{3a} ~~restores the neutrality of X_1 while~~
DISPLAYS
~~retaining~~ the distinction between center and edge in both plan and elevation.
AND THE DISTINCTION BETWEEN SIDE A AND SIDE B

A_{3c}
VOLUME(S)   SOLID AND CUBE
X_{3c} Superimposition of X_3 and X_{3a} with resultant edge cubes treated as ~~solid~~
~~and the center cruciform as void.~~

A_{3d}
X_{3d} ~~Reversal of X_{3c}. Center solid; edge cubes void.~~

House IV, transcript of operations, Peter Eisenman, undated

YALE UNIVERSITY
NEW HAVEN · CONNECTICUT · 06520

DEPARTMENT OF COMPARATIVE LITERATURE
1115 BINGHAM HALL

très solide ressemblerait à la fois à une trame, à
un crible ou une grille (GRID) et
à un instrument de musique à corde (CHORD).
(piano, harpe, lyre?)

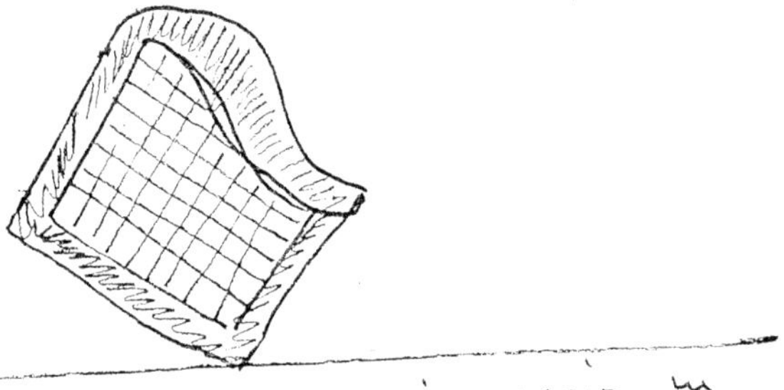

En tant que grille, grid, etc., il aurait un
certain rapport avec le filtre interprétatif et
sélectif qu'aura pu être le lieu et le crible
les 3 sites et les 3 couches (IDE, BT, CV) etc.
En tant qu'instrument à la corde, il ferait
figurer la chora de choral work.

~~Peut-être~~ Je crois que rien ne devrait être
inscrit sur cette sculpture, à moins que, peut-être,
quelques lettres et une signature n'y figurent quelque
part (Choral works, by ... -1986 ...) - A discuter,
entre autres choses.

Letter from Jacques Derrida to Peter Eisenman, 1987, published in *Chora L Works*, 1997

"writing … cannot be subsumed under concepts whose contours it draws, leaves only its ghost to a logic that can only seek to govern it insofar as logic arises from it … "[15] In *Inside Form*Z*, a guidebook to that software published in 2000, author Eden Greig Muir explains that since the software requires forms to be created through Boolean operations on precursor forms, those first objects must be subsequently "ghosted" out of renderings, or eventually cleared or rendered inactive. The guidebook's prosaic programmatic language has a kind of inadvertent yet relevant poetry: "'The Clear All Ghosted' command deletes all inactive (ghosted) objects in your project. Ghosted objects are not usually as valuable as active objects. Nevertheless … if a particular ghosted object is valuable to you, unghost it and place it on a separate inactive layer."[16]

1. Barbara Isenberg, *Conversations with Frank Gehry* (New York, 2009), p. 172.
2. Bernard Tschumi, "Introduction," in *Chora L Works, Jacques Derrida and Peter Eisenman* (New York, 1997), p. 125.
3. Roland Barthes, "Death of the Author," in *Image, Music Text/Roland Barthes; Essays Selected and Translated by Stephen Heath* (New York, 1977), p. 142.
4. Peter Eisenman, "Misreading," in *Houses of Cards* (New York, 1987), p. 186
5. Nicholas Negroponte, *The Architecture Machine: Towards a More Humane Environment*, (Cambridge, MA, 1970). p. ii.
6. Ibid, p. 9.
7. Greg Lynn, *Animate Form*, (New York, 1999), p. 10.
8. This and subsequent Lynn quotations: Greg Lynn, in conversation with Thomas de Monchaux, November 2013.
9. Mark Rappolt and Robert Violette, eds., *Gehry Draws* (Cambridge, MA, 2004), p. 92.
10. Philip Johnson and Mark Wigley, *Deconstructivist Architecture* (Boston, 1988), p. 56.
11. Mildred Friedman, ed., *Gehry Talks: Architecture + Process* (New York, 1999) p. 52.
12. Rappolt and Violette 2004 (see note 9), p. 22.
13. Isenberg 2009 (see note 1), p. 90.
14. *Tschumi on Architecture: Conversations with Enrique Walker* (New York, 2006), p. 55.
15. Mark Wigley, *The Architecture of Deconstruction: Derrida's Haunt* (Cambridge, MA, 1995), p. 193.
16. Eden Greig Muir, *Inside Form*Z: Guide to 3D Modeling and Rendering* (Albany, New York, 2000), p. 324.

Maison de Verre
Kenneth Frampton

In the Maison de Verre one is confronted with a work which defies any accepted form of classification. It is not merely a question of an inability to place it from a stylistic or conceptual point of view. The genre of the work itself is problematic. Are we to regard it as a building in the accepted sense or should we rather think of it as a grossly enlarged piece of furniture, interjected into an altogether larger realm? The site plan reveals this realm, as an elongated building lot, integral to the residential infrastructure of eighteenth-century Paris. The Maison de Verre is an insertion into this lot both horizontally and vertically and thus it is more probably correct to regard it as a large furnishing element rather than as simply a house in the conventional sense. This precious distinction acquires greater validity once one realizes that Pierre Chareau was, by temperament and training, more concerned with interiors than with exteriors. It is further substantiated by the relative banality of Chareau's freestanding buildings. One cannot recognize the golf club built at Beauvallon in 1927 to the designs of Chareau and Bijvoet, as being a work, by the same team who produced the Maison de Verre.

There is no demonstrable conscious link between Paul Scheerbart's Glasarchitektur of 1914 and the Maison de Verre. Nonetheless the Maison de Verre curiously echoes, however unconsciously, Scheerbart's prophetic vision. It embodies an altogether richer and more total realization of this vision than either he or his professional alter ego Bruno Taut were ever to achieve. Between Taut's glass pavilion dedicated to Scheerbart and built for the Deutsche Werkbund Ausstellung of 1914 and Chareau's Maison de Verre, no structures exist in which glass lenses were used as the prime protective skin. Auguste Perret naturally had the audacity to use glass lenses as early as 1903, as cladding to the stair shaft of his famous Rue Franklin apartments. As a general walling technique however, they made a relatively late entry into the vocabulary of twentieth-century architecture.[1] This delay, despite Taut's versatile demonstration of 1914, was no doubt due in part to a certain technical insecurity. Even as late as 1929, St. Gobain was still unprepared to give a weatherproof guarantee to the proposed use of lenses in the Maison de Verre. It is a measure of Chareau's clients' courage that they were willing to adopt such an unproven material for the enclosure of their house.[2]

Iconographically, glass lenses had long been anticipated, first by Mackintosh and then in the work of the Viennese school. Both Hoffmann and Loos made extensive use of square gridded areas of glass throughout their work. This glazing device, derived from Japan, was consciously employed by late Art Nouveau architects in order to increase the area of glazing and at the same time to emphasize the surface of transparent planes. Thus used to much the same end, the glass lenses in the Maison de Verre, largely account for the Oriental atmosphere that pervades the house. Mackintosh's Glasgow School of Art Library of 1907 and Hoffmann's Palais Stoclet, Brussels of 1905 are both prototypical in respect to such planar emphasis, while a typical contemporary Viennese example is Loos' Michaelerplatz department store of 1910. In the Michaelerplatz store, as in the Glasgow School of Art, gridded glass is projected into the frontal plane where it occupies a position usually reserved for massive construction. In further anticipation of the Maison de Verre the gridded glazed planes of this store are pierced with opening lights of clear glass.

It is obvious that the Viennese school and in particular, Hoffmann's pupil, Gabriel Guvrekian and to a greater extent Adolf Loos, exercised a considerable influence on Chareau's development. Apart from the mutual friendship of all three men during the period of Loos' extended sojourn in Paris, during the nineteen-twenties, the similarity of their separate approaches to the problem of the domestic interior is testimony in itself. Guvrekian's interior for his Villa Heim of 1926 and Loos' Moller House, Vienna of 1928 are very parallel, at least stylistically to Chareau's project for an embassy suite displayed at the *Exposition des Arts Decoratifs* in 1925.

Despite his polemical radicalism Loos maintained an

Pierre Chareau, embassy suite, Exposition des Arts Decoratifs, Paris, 1925

allegiance to bourgeois values which found direct symbolic expression in his predilection for hard wearing traditional materials, such as teak or walnut paneling, parquet flooring and marble. This *revetment* symbolism appears to have influenced the stylistic point of departure of the Parisian Union des Artistes Moderne, founded in 1929, by René Herbst, Pierre Chareau, Francis Jourdain, Hélene Henry, Rob Mallet-Stevens, Charlotte Perriand, and Sonia Delaunay, amongst many others. The UAM artists however introduced a much lighter touch into the Loosian vocabulary, a tendency deriving partially out of Hoffmann and Voysey, partially out of cubism and particularly out of a French preoccupation with ingenuity and invention for its own sake. This development was somewhat at variance with Loos' haute couture taste. By the late twenties however, the UAM group had freed itself from the influence of measured ostentation in favor of a preference for modest interiors of plywood furniture and off white walls. The eccentric Loosian juxtaposition of rustic *Style Anglais* with neoclassical luxury found its aesthetic resolution in this UAM development, in the simple homogeneity of Jourdain's severe interiors and,

as a one-off piece, in the rich articulation of material in Chareau's Maison de Verre.

All the same the high bourgeois style of Loos conditioned the material aura of the Maison de Verre, even if it in no way determined its organization, which arose directly out of Chareau's inventiveness and Bijvoet's sense of order. Chareau, in conjunction with his *artisanat* Dalbet, had literally begun to invent his *poésie d'équipage* as early as 1918, when he designed the interior of a two room St. Germain apartment for a young doctor and his wife, Doctor and Madame Dalsace, who were later to become the clients of the Maison de Verre.[3] Chareau's penchant for invention was fundamental to the final form of the house, as were the peculiar circumstances under which it was eventually to be achieved.

In 1928 Madame Dalsace's father bought an eighteenth-century town house in 31 Rue St. Guillame. The property was flanked on both sides by party walls of varying height and comprised in addition to an existing three-story house, a small forecourt and a garden in the rear. Initially the clients had every intention of demolishing the existing house and building anew but the presence of an uncooperative old lady in residence on the second floor, secure as a protected tenant under law, compelled both client and architect to devise a new solution. This impasse led to the perhaps inevitable but nonetheless daring decision to permanently underpin the existing second floor with steel. The subsequent demolition of the unoccupied floors spared only the staircase access to the existing second floor. This residual feature, asymmetrically located, afforded the only distortion in a volume which was otherwise a clear rectilinear roofed over space extending from fore court to garden. This volume possessed sufficient elevation to comfortably accommodate three new floors of normal height. Consequently three new levels were provided, each one being devoted to a different activity. The ground floor was allocated to medical practice, the first floor to "public" and "semi-public" space and the second floor to private sleeping space, bedrooms, bathrooms, etc. A three-story service wing, comprising kitchen and maids quarters was built out from the main volume to one side of the forecourt. Once this shell was complete, it only remained to organize these levels in detail and "to envelop the necessities of the house."[4] For this purpose glass lenses were selected for their translucent property, which afforded both privacy and light. Of this mutual decision of client and architect to totally glaze the house Dr. Dalsace has written as follows:

Thanks to an old lady who did not wish to leave her sordid apartment on the second floor, Pierre Chareau realized a structural tour de force of three luminous floors, within the ground floor and the first floor of this small town house. These two floors had been so dark that the employees of the old lady, who would live to be a hundred, were obliged to work throughout the day by artificial light. Light permeates freely, around this block, of which the ground floor is given over to medicine, the first floor to social life and the second to nocturnal habitation. The problem thus posed was enormously difficult to resolve. The interpenetration of rooms, some which ran through two floors (i.e. consultation room and hall) made the problem of sound insulation very difficult .... The ground floor, the professional section of the house, facilitates work and affords to the patients, once their first anxiety is over, great calmness. The whole house was created under the sign of amity, in perfect affective accord.[5]

These words of Dr. Dalsace are very revealing or they indicate with great economy, the nature of the close collaboration that occurred between these exceptionally cultured clients and their architect. In referring to the first floor as being designated to *la vie de societe*, Dr. Dalsace makes it clear that this level was from the outset thought of, as being unusually public. It was not simply a *salle de sejour*. It is this initial central concept of a large public salon flooded with light, which no doubt now accounts for one's invariable experience of this house as a "world within a world," enclosing its own hierarchy of public and private spaces. The light diffusing through the salon walls simulates a quality of illumination comparable to that experienced in the open air and this condition is maintained at night, when the interior of the house is again illuminated by light, diffusing through the glass lenses of its *pan verre*, from floodlights mounted off the forecourt and garden façades. One cannot but recall Scheerbart's words of 1914. "In order to raise our culture to a higher level, we are forced, whether we like it or not, to change our architecture. And this will be possible only if we free the rooms in which we live of their enclosed

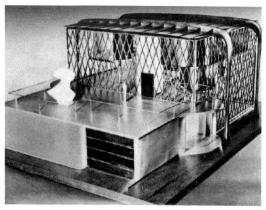

La Maison Suspendue, photograph of maquette

characters. This, however, we can only do by introducing a glass architecture which admits the light of the sun, of the moon, and of the stars, not only through a few windows, but through as many walls as feasible, these to consist entirely of glass—of colored glass."[6] And later of the artificial illumination of such a house, from within its double walls of glass he wrote: "This kind of lighting would make the entire glass house into a huge lantern which can glow on quiet summer nights like glow worms and fireflies."[7] Today the light radiating from the Maison de Verre at night, concretises this pioneer vision.

Early interior perspectives of this house indicate that details of its subdivision were finalized during the course of its construction. These naïve drawings are the only evidence we have as to the nature of its invention and fabrication. They suggest that once the main concept was established the total work evolved like a montage, stage by stage and element by element.[8] A maquette of the house, exhibited as late as 1931 shows a definite stage in this development. From the outset the commission was exploited as an opportunity for evolving a technically determined environment rather than as an occasion for simply another piece of domestic design. Both the materials and techniques adopted were redolent with industrial potential, even although the methods of actual realization were far from industrial.[9] It is clear for instance, that the demonstrative use of bent duralumin somewhere in the house was envisaged from the outset. In an early project sketch the balustrade to the main stair is shown as being fabricated out of this material. It was finally realized in tubular steel—bent duralumin re-emerging as a material-form in the master bathroom storage-space dividers and in the cylindrical broom cupboard. Thus a "poetry of technique"—pervaded the whole house and must prevail over any simple functional interpretation of its conception and realization. In this respect, the projected mobile book cabinets in the main salon perspective, were in their context, more of a poetic idea, than they were a reasonable solution to the problem of book storage. Here we have a pure example of image preceding idea in the design process, a procedure that is now an anathema to today's methodical designers. In this instance, the initial "image-idea" became transformed into two mobile pieces of equipment situated at either end of the salon: the one, the suspended dumb waiter, running from the kitchen to the dining area, (forever to remain incomplete) and the other, the mobile access ladder to the double height book wall. Herein a metaphorical mobility becomes ironically balanced, the two units dispensing physical and spiritual food respectively.

The invention of the Maison de Verre may be characterized under three separate but interrelated aspects, articulation, transformation and transparency.

Through the articulation and standardization of its components the house acquires implications that extend outside the confines of its domestic scale. Limited in its actual prefabrication, it nonetheless postulates, through its modular order, a world of high quality mass production. Doors, balustrades, book racks, storage units, and fenestration are all treated as modular components of a grid, running through the house from front to back and in limited sections from side to side.

The apparent "elementarism" of this articulation is due in part no doubt to the influence of Frank Lloyd Wright, whose presence is clearly in evidence in the early work of Bijvoet and Duiker. Bijvoet for his part has recently denied that he was ever under the influence of Rietveld, although he was certainly aware of his work. This being so any Neoplastic influence must be largely discounted. There remains of course Kiesler's *Cité dans L'Espace* which, built for the 1925 *Exposition des Arts Decoratifs*, would have presented to an aware Parisian audience, an "elementarism" of constructivist origin.[10] One final implication of the articulated order of the Maison de Verre is

that its component units are not only modular but in essence interchangeable; yielding a "mobility" dependent upon a potential for modification and replacement rather than movement per se.

The Maison de Verre is the transformable plan *par excellence*: "transformable" to such a degree that the *raison d'être* of its transformation ranges from necessity, to convenience, to subtle poetic variation. The pivotal radial door to the landing of the main stair is necessary for the separation of the private accommodation from the medical suite, while the sliding wall to the salon conveniently isolates the doctor's study from the main living space. Many other examples of necessary transformation clearly abound; however, poetic variations in small-scale components, occur throughout the house and these are largely provided in order to achieve subtle changes in light and transparency. The components of the house are thus often articulated into "primary," "secondary," and "tertiary" elements and it is the latter that usually provides this final degree of lyrical variation. It is the perforated metal "butterfly" screens for instance which transform the main stair enclosure from a condition of transparency, to one of translucence. A very similar but functionally even less justifiable variation to the degree of enclosure is built into the screening of the garden entrance door.

In contrast to the Rietveld-Schroeder House of 1924, the one classic transformable plan to which it may be readily compared, the mobile space dividers of the Maison de Verre frequently only modify the basic character of the available space, rather than effect a total transformation. In this respect, the folding screens which determines the limits of the patients' waiting area, provide a partial (i.e. visual) transformation of the space. On the other hand, the frameless pivoting story-height doors and sliding wall panels have a capacity to radically alter the spaces in which they are located.

The walls of the Maison de Verre are predominantly translucent. Hence its composition is ordered primarily through a transparency that is phenomenal rather than literal. In its interior, it is inherently organized as a series of vertical planes or layers of space proceeding frontally from the forecourt towards the garden. That this was the initial design intention is suggested by the treatment and arrangement of the columns and column axes. The main

Second-floor interior view of the house under construction, 1930

floor slabs of the house are cantilevered beyond the column system on both the front and rear façades. In each instance, the row of columns immediately adjacent to the cantilever have their web axes aligned parallel to the elevations, that is, directly at right angles to the web axes of the interior columns. As a counterchange this establishes "slots" of space immediately behind the façade and these "slots" naturally stress the transverse plane and induce a reading of similar stratified layers throughout the remaining space.

In their essay[11] on literal and phenomenal transparency Colin Rowe and Robert Slutsky submit that similar stratifications of space are to be perceived in Le Corbusier's Villa Garches of 1927, wherein planar recessions occur not only as vertical phenomena but also horizontally in plan. It may be argued that almost exactly parallel conditions pertain in the Maison de Verre where horizontal planes are deliberately displaced over each other, partly to emphasize certain areas, and partly to create a deflecting cubistic "rift" in the spatial expression. This

split in level not only subdivides the space but also affords a directional transition between the implied shallow spaces adjacent to each of the façades and the overall depth of the total volume. In the Villa Garches, the floor levels remain constant and a comparable spatial modulation is achieved through the use of freestanding elements. This geological fault as it were, in the Maison de Verre, runs laterally from front to back on the ground and first floors and is even echoed in the organization of the garden. It also finds complementary expression in the façades of the house. On the forecourt façade it manifests itself as a subtle displacement to the lowest course of glass lenses; a "break" which is precisely reflected in the articulation of the entrance foyer roof. On the garden façade it appears as a much more complex overlap of "transparent" planes, laterally displaced—a series of projections and counter projections which mutually occur in respect to the main translucent façade, comprising the project curtain wall of Mme. Dalsace's day room and the cantilevered bedroom terrace above. On each façade

Main stair entry

these "overlaps" receive their most articulate expression in the detailing of the steel framed glazing. Thus Mme. Dalsace's conservatory is consistently treated as a first floor version of the forecourt entrance foyer. In spite of this consistency, the fundamental contrast between the garden and forecourt façades, between dynamism and restraint, serves to remind us of a similar contrast of expression to be found in the Villa Garches.

Out of an attempt to emphasize such spatial displacements, horizontally, as well as out of a need to provide appropriate functional surfaces, a number of contrasting floor finishes have been applied throughout the house. Thus a studded off-white tile is used throughout the active public spaces, a small black ceramic tile is used in the semi-public quiet places, a wooden strip tile surfaces the dining area and the gallery, while an off-white ceramic tile is applied to the kitchen and the medical examination suite. These different floor materials are combined together in a manner highly reminiscent of synthetic cubist collage. Changes in surface finish announce

either changes in "use" or space definitive non-utilitarian changes in the floor level. Finally it should be noted that an atypical crank in the slab occurs in the second floor, which although it stresses the transverse space serves primarily as a structural anchor to the terrace which cantilevers beyond.

The mechanization of the Maison de Verre was extensive and (such was the caliber of Dalbet's craftsmanship) economically conceived and precisely executed. In many of the details the strength of the material used is pushed to its limits. Typical of this is the mobile book wall ladder, which travels on a carriage made out of a single bent metal tube. The remote controlled steel louvers to the salon and the opening lights of the main façades are thus by no means the only éléments-méchanique type de la maison.[12] On the contrary mobility permeates, every detail of this house, from adjustable mirrors to pivoting closets. Even the system of servicing the house seems to have been conditioned by this concern for mobility. Thus throughout the house all wiring, power, light, telephone, etc. is conveyed vertically through free standing tubes, rising from floor to floor. These tubes mount control consoles in which all outlets and switches are located; thus relieving the walls of this task. In the same manner as these tubes carry power and light, the floor slabs carry heat in the form of ducted air, emitted from raised outlets set in the floor. This combined servicing system is open to being read as horizontal planes carrying heat in the form of conditioned air, pierced at intervals by vertical lines carrying power and light.

The "functionalism" of the Maison de Verre is permeated by such metaphorical ideas at every level. A great deal of its equipment and mechanization is poetic and symbolic rather than strictly functional. Thus the provision of bidets is "symbolically" in excess of the amount that could be conceivably required by the program, on the grounds of hygiene. The lateral mobility of these elements serves only to emphasize yet further their ironic profusion in the house of a gynecologist. Save for its highly rudimentary kitchen the Maison de Verre was a total demonstration of a "complete" architectural vocabulary. To this end it became the vehicle for five distinctly different solutions to the problem of the stair. From a retractable ship's companion ladder, to a stringless stair structurally integral with its balustrade, to the articulated tread of the main stair bracketed off steel string beams, each stairway link was made the occasion for a different approach. The result was the building out of a possible technical repertoire *à la Neufert*. The next generation would bring certain elements of this repertoire a step nearer to general adoption by the society at large. The work of the French "artisan-engineer" Jean Prouvé represents the most direct practical continuation of this line. In this context Prouvé's work since 1935 and in particular his present curtain wall designs may be regarded as extended, independent developments of the curtain wall railway carriage window type first prototyped in the Maison de Verre.

The relation between the Maison de Verre and the architectural tradition of which it is a part is as complex as it is elusive. The work and thought of Le Corbusier must have played an important role in its conception. Bernard Bijvoet, on his own admission, was under the influence of Le Corbusier at this time, as was his Dutch partner Johannes Duiker. This partnership had displayed immediate post war affinities with the work of Wright, but

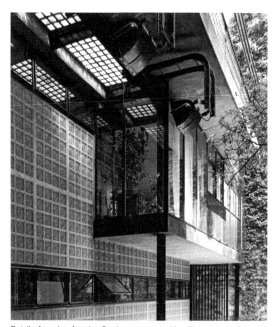

Detail of garden façade. Garden entrance with grill gate is in the rear ground. Madame Dalsace's day room and conservatory project outward at first floor level. Lense lights are set into the second-floor bedroom terrace overhead, with night floodlighting also suspended from this level.

during the late twenties appears to have veered towards a European *Neue Sachlichken* position. In any event Le Corbusier's Five Points of a New Architecture first published in 1926, certainly appears to have influenced the basic conception of the house—three of these points finding very definite expression in its form: *le plan libre; la façade libre, and la fenêtre en longeur.*[13] After the completion of the house at the end of 1931, there is sufficient evidence of it having some counter influence on the work of Le Corbusier. Le Corbusier's Immeuble Clarté built in Geneva in 1932 has virtue of its glass lenses, its glass stair treads, its indirect lighting, its fenestration, and its transformable plans, definite affinities with the Maison de Verre.[14]

Similar characteristics are to be found in the detailing of Le Corbusier's own apartment house built at Porte Molitor, Paris, in 1933. One may argue of course that this "syntax" had already been partially anticipated by Perriand and Le Corbusier themselves in their joint interior exhibit for the Salon d'Automne of 1929.[15]

In spite of its caliber the Maison de Verre did not exert an extensive influence on the next generation. At the time of its completion it was well received by the yellow press as a curiosity, and partly criticized by the professional press, for being too utopian, intellectual, and insufficiently utilitarian.[16]

Thus it became at once part of an underground tradition; its immediate influence limited to a select few who were sympathetic to its creation. Le Corbusier was of course a member of the *coterie*, but no other member of the main stream seems to have been either aware of or touched by its achievement. Bijvoet of course carried its presence to Holland, when he returned home after Duiker's death in 1934, to complete the Hotel Gooiland in Hilversum. The rich materials adopted in its foyer detailing and the transformable nature of its public space, jointly suggest a Parisian attitude in this hotel design that can only be attributed to Bijvoet.

Of the next generation only the young Parisian architect Paul Nelson appears to have been profoundly influenced by the unique conception of the Maison de Verre. Above all else, Nelson appears to have been impressed by its creation of a world within a world, the internal realm being all but totally isolated from the outside by a continuous translucent membrane. This notion of isolation

View of main salon, at night, with external lighting from second-floor gallery; note travelling book wall stair. The easy chair and settee are by Chareau and finished in fabric by Andre Lurcat.

General view of the salon. Armchairs are according to designs by Pierre Chareau

was first developed by Nelson in his project for a hospital facility at Ismalia for the Suez Canal Company designed in 1936.[17] Here the external isolation took the form of a continuous independent sun screening envelope—Nelson's *envelope parasolaire* within which the hospital surgical facility was to have been housed. This facility itself also comprised in its turn a world within a world, for Nelson incorporated within it for the first time, his invention on an ovoid operating theater, of the type that he was eventually to realize in his Franco-American hospital at St. Louis. In fact, there was a whole hierarchy of Chinese boxes in Nelson's Ismalia project: firstly, the four ovoid theaters, secondly, their surrounding service space, thirdly, the hospital proper and finally, the total *brise-soleil* envelope. Nelson followed this study in isolation with his famous 1936-37 project for a Maison Suspendue, which was to be his most direct development of the concepts embodied in the Maison de Verre.

La Maison Suspendue was directly parallel to the Maison de Verre in its program. It too, could only have been erected in the service of an elite, even if such an elite was envisaged as no longer being a bourgeois elite, but rather an elite of a new collective society. Nelson's own analysis of the spatial order of his project, into ground floor service level, second floor living level and first floor non-utilitarian leisure space, directly reflects the organization of the Maison de Verre. In this respect Nelson's commentary on the Maison Suspendue could be applied just as equally to the Maison de Verre. In 1937 he wrote: "The principle of isolating the individual suggests at once the idea of a closed form in contrast to the open form of collective architecture," (and) … "because the principle of its enrichment suggests an architecture which develops itself in the interior of this closed form" (there is a)— "contrast to the traditional house wherein the elevation plays the major role." For Nelson this concept yields, "an architecture in which the spiritual needs of man become predominant in a new space which one may term "useless," in comparison with the purely utilitarian space of material needs—(in) contrast to rational architecture."[18]

In this brief outline resides not only the paradox of the Maison de Verre and the Maison Suspendue, but also the final paradox of the work and thought of Pierre Chareau and the end of the curious problematic nature of a twentieth-century architectural tradition as a whole. For Chareau, as many other twentieth-century designers, created his finest work, in the service of an elite bourgeoisie, yet he printed, as is clear from his essay "La Création Artistique et l'Imitation Commerciale," to place his services at the disposal of the society as a whole.[19]

In an age of population explosion and shelter scarcity, the minimal dwelling of a "rational architecture" for which Nelson implied a certain contempt can now no doubt be the only initial standard for domestic building in a class society. In spite of our much-proclaimed influence, the inundations of our consumer industry and the deprivations of our military waste render elusive an optimum adequate level of environment for all. As a general system the Maison de Verre is technically feasible but in societal-spatial terms, economically unattainable. What, in the thirties, could have been construed as a belated one-off realization of technical utopianism, now appears as a utopianism of space. In our present circumstances, *une abondance d'espace inutile*[20] can have substance only as the motivating ideal of some future nonrepressive society. The general realization of such lavish spatial standards would involve a major reallocation of resources and an unimaginable degree of technicalization. All the same the conscious attempt to elevate the scale of a home into that of a palace, (a line evoked by Le Corbusier), projects the program of a dwelling out of the private domestic realm to a myth of collectivity wherein the house becomes a prototypical *palais du peuple.* How a private bourgeois residence could come to acquire even some of these public and collective connotations remains as yet one of the cultural paradoxes of the twentieth century. It is curious that, thirty-seven years later its erection, a purpose-made house should still have a capacity to exert a powerful influence on our imagination. Perhaps, it is because it continues to offer through the fluidity of its plan, the standardization of its components and the mobility of its parts and through its clear assembly of public and private spaces within a single envelope, a general model from which to evolve solutions to some of the indeterminate problems of our epoch.

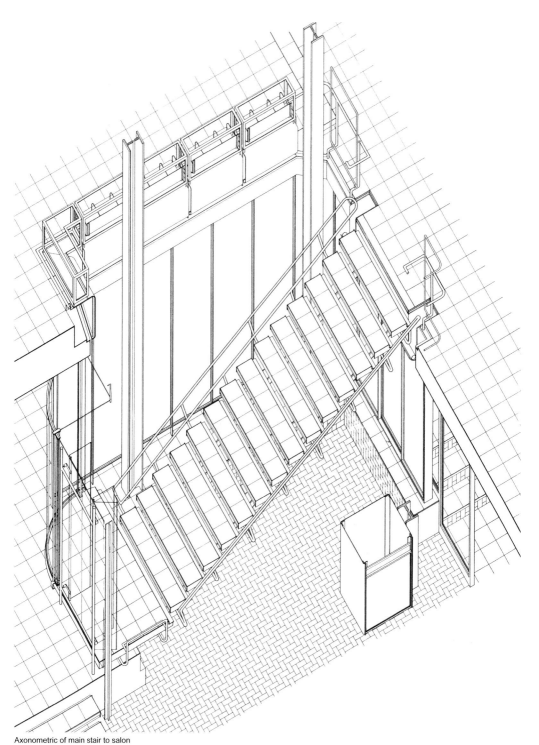

Axonometric of main stair to salon

1. tunnel entrance 12
2. forecourt
3. 2-car garage
4. existing eighteenth-century building
5. entrance to house
6. entrance to house above
7. service wing
8. garden access
9. consulting room terrace
10. ground ivy
11. grass and shrubs
12. gravel play court

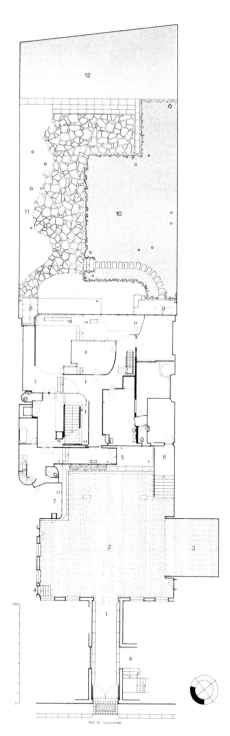

Site plan with ground floor

Pierre Chareau

Pierre Chareau was born into a Le Havre ship-owning family in 1883. He studied in Paris and at seventeen hesitated between painting, music, and architecture. He decided in favor of a career as a decorator and entered the Paris branch of the famous English furnishing firm Waring & Gillow, where he remained for four years. With the outbreak of war in 1914 he entered military service.

In 1918 he designed the interior of a St. Germain apartment for the Dalsace family, who later became his clients for the Maison de Verre. Furniture pieces for this commission were subsequently exhibited at the Salon d'Automne of 1919, an event that brought Chareau recognition.

Chareau met Dalbet at this time and the two men became collaborators. During the twenties Chareau produced numerous interior pieces in collaboration with artists such as Jean Lurçat, Hélène Henry, Jacques Lipchitz, and his wife Dollie Pierre Chareau.

For the famous *Exposition des Arts Decoratifs* of 1925 he designed an embassy suite that revealed his interests in indirect lighting, in mechanism and in traditional rich materials. On this occasion he met Bijvoet and persuaded him to leave Holland and join him in Paris; thus together they designed in 1926 Chareau's first and only free standing work of any size, the golf clubhouse for Monsieur Bernheim, the father of Mme. Dalsace.

By 1927 they were again at work on a reception hall for a hotel at Tours and in the following year they began their first studies for the Maison de Verre. The Maison de Verre was finally completed at the beginning of 1932. In 1932 Chareau realized a suite of offices for the L.T.T. Paris, a design that was gauche compared to the Dalsace house. After this commission came the full impact of the depression. In the general dearth of work, Chareau suffered more than most of his colleagues and it was this no doubt that partly provoked his bitter essay, "La Création Artistique et l'Imitation Commerciale," published in September 1935.

Chareau continued to produce small pieces for the UAM exhibitions, but even these made little impression. In 1937 he designed a house for Djemel Anik and in 1938 an equally unknown work for the French Foreign Ministry. After his emigration to America in 1939 he designed a studio for Robert Motherwell at East Hampton, Long Island, plus two small houses in the vicinity, one of which he occupied on completion. He died in 1950, in East Hampton.

Originally published in Perspecta 12, The Yale Architectural Journal, *1969, pp. 77—128. Reprinted with permission.*

1. Glass lenses do not occur to any extent in Le Corbusier's work until his first project for the Armée du Salut of 1929.

2. As I have remarked elsewhere both the Maison de Verre and the Rietveld Schröder house involved the direct patronage of highly cultivated women. See *Arena, Journal of the Architectural Association*, London, April, 1966, pp. 257–62.

3. See *Decorative Art 1933, Yearbook of "The Studio,"* London, p. 113. This commission involved Chareau in the design and construction of two pieces of furniture, a bed and a desk, which were subsequently exhibited in the Salon d'Automne of 1919, an event that established Chareau's reputation as a designer. Pierre Chareau first met Dalbet through working on purpose-made pieces of this kind, Dalbet was a type of artisan very comparable to Gerrit Rietveld.

4. Viollet-le-Duc, *Entretiens sur l'Architecture*.

5. Rene Herbst, *Pierre Chareau*, Editions du Salon des Arts Ménagers, Union des Artistes Modernes, Paris 1954, pp. 7–8.

6. Paul Scheerbart, *Glasarchitektur*, Berlin, Verlag der Sturm, 1914, p. 11 (Translation by C.C. & G.R. Collins).

7. Op. cit., p. 48.

8. Bernard Bijvoet has recently confirmed in an interview with Robert Vickery that no proper working drawings were ever prepared for the house.

9. Nevertheless, according to Julien Lepage (see footnote 16) Chareau consciously regarded the house, "as a model realized by artisans with a view to industrial standardization."

10. See Henry van der Velde, "Die Pariser Kunstgewerbeaustellung." Republished in *Werk*, No. 2, February 1965, pp. 59–60. Apart from Kiesler's work and Le Corbusier's Pavillion L'Esprit Nouveau, the Peter Behren's greenhouse for this exhibition is also to be regarded as having been influential.

11. Colin Rowe and Robert Slutsky, "Transparency Literal and Phenomenal," *Perspecta No. 8, Yale School of Architecture Magazine*, 1964, pp. 45–54.

12. A phrase coined by Le Corbusier and Pierre Jeanneret in their, "Cinq Poins d'une Architecture Nouvelle," 1926.

13. Le Corbusier et Pierre Jeanneret, *Oeuvre Complete, 1910-1929*, 8th Edition, Les Editions d'Architecture, Girsberger, Zurich, 1965, pp. 128 & 129.

14. See Stani von Moos, "Aspekte der Neuen Architektur in Paris 1912–1932," *Werk*, No. 2, February 1965, pp. 52–56.

15. Le Corbusier et Pierre Jeanneret, *Oeuvre Complete, 1929–1934*, 6th Edition, Editions Girsberger, Zurich 1957, pp 42–46.

16. See L'Architecture d'Aujourd'hui, No. 9. November / December 1933, pp. 4–15. This was the first full-length documentation of the Maison de Verre with critical appraisals by Pierre Vago, Paul Nelson and Julien Lepage. Some of Lepage's comments were very perceptive and are worth quoting. He wrote: "Above all one notices the same care to make visible and express every possible function and not only to acknowledge the real needs of the owner, but even to organize all his possible needs and to arouse in him and to satisfy in advance new desires, which he has not yet thought of." And again of the mechanical aspects of the house Lepage wrote: "In this sense however there is nothing mechanistic about this house. None of the equipment is menacing. It is all treated with such delicacy and its function is so well revealed that all these pieces are more like organs than instruments. Elsewhere he wrote: "It is astonishing to see how the architect by inserting more, or less transparent windows in the translucent brick skin of the house is able to evoke a character which is alternately, intimate, free and livable in the bedrooms, the official reception and patient's waiting area; precise and scientific, in the consulting room and soft and feminine in the boudoir suspended over the garden." This was in strict contrast to Vago's critique, for whom the house was too mechanistic to be considered as a general solution. Thus Vago rhetorically demands "It is indispensable for men of the twentieth century to spend their days, their hours, of leisure and rest in a glass box, among randomly placed columns, with their rivets exposed, in a laboratory open on all sides... to receive the roast on a suspended wagon, to enter one's room via a mobile ladder ..."

17. *Deux Etudes Hospitalieres par Paul Nelson*, Editions Morance, Paris, 1934. (See Pavillon de Chirurgie – d'un groupe hospitalier en pays chaud, Ismalia, 1936.)

18. Paul Nelson, *La Maison Suspendue*, Editions Morance, Paris, 1937. In this document Nelson postulates the Maison Suspendue as being in strict opposition to the "rational-collective" architecture; the *existenzminimum* of the socialist technocratic architects of the thirties.

19. See *L'Architecture d'Aujourd'hui*, No. 9, September 1935, pp. 68–69. In this highly charged essay Chareau testifies to his position. He writes: "Architecture is a social art. It is at one and the same time a consummation of all the arts and an emanation of the masses. The architect can only create if he listens to and understands the voices of millions of men, if he shares in their sufferings, if he struggles with them for their freedom, if he becomes the precentor of their hopes, the realizer of their aspirations. He uses the iron that they forge. He gives life to the theories they conceive. He helps them to live, to produce, to create, to consume. He guides them toward the future because he is aware of that which belongs to the past. Indeed he lives only for them. Architecture is determined by the lives of these men. It can choose to either lead, deceive, or mesmerize them."

20. Ibid.

Maison de Verre*

Paul Nelson

Bernard Bijvoet was born in 1889 in The Hague. He was educated in The Hague and then at the Technical University of Delft where he graduated in 1913 as a *Boukundig Engenieur*. In Delft he met Johannes Duiker and after graduation they worked together for Professor Evers and on competitions.

In 1917 Bijvoet and Duiker were successful in a competition for old people's housing in Alkmaar and on the strength of this they established their partnership. In 1918 they were again premiated for their design for the Rijksacademie of Fine Arts. During the early twenties Duiker and Bijvoet were strongly influenced by Wright. The Dutch Neoplastic movement curiously enough was never an influence on their work. By 1924 however with the realization of their remarkable Aalsmeer House, they had acquired a totally different, almost Neue Sachlichkeit, orientation.

In 1925 Bijvoet met Chareau in Paris at the Exhibition, where the Duiker/Bijvoet entries for the Rijksacademie and the Chicago Tribune were being exhibited. The depressing Dutch economic situation encouraged Bijvoet to remain in Paris and to work as an associate of Chareau. After the completion of the Maison de Verre in 1932 Bijvoet left Chareau to work with Beaudoin and later with Nelson.

In 1934, on Duiker's death, he returned to Holland to complete the work which Duiker had initiated on the Hotel Gooiland, Hilversum. During the late thirties he worked with Holt in Haarlem and afterwards spent the war years in the Dordogne. He now lives in The Hague where he continues to run an extensive practice.

The present epoch has created a life of new awareness and reflexes, but architecture has not evolved sufficiently to be able to express it; for it cannot be expressed only by a detail or a façade, nor by ironmongery or through the use of certain materials, nor by the use of such clichés as horizontal or vertical windows. It is discouraging to observe this decorative application of *moderne*, changed in accordance with fashion, to dress up the most *pompiers* of pompier buildings and to alight upon these so-called "pure" buildings which, like a poster, have nothing in common with the advertised product. There is another task for contemporary architecture,

possibly less spectacular, wherein the philosophical awareness of the architect allows for the spiritual and physical program of this new life to be established and for its expression in plan and where the knowledge of building technique permits this plan to be realized so that it works. A Parisian doctor has given Chareau a chance to attempt this task.

Amplification is the essential characteristic of this new life. Since the invention of the bicycle established an epoch, man has extended the amplification of his powers through mechanical means: the telephone, the telegraph and the automobile are all conquests in two dimensions, while the airplane, the radio and the television are conquests in three. The house must then be a machine which amplifies our sensation of life. Man today has an awareness of space and, to an even greater extent, of movement in space. A study in plan and section no longer affords the architect the means by which to fulfill and represent his requirements: the fourth dimension, time, intervenes. One must create spaces which have to be passed through in a relative lapse of time. One must feel the fourth dimension. This house in Rue St. Guillaume incites this sensation.

One has begun at the outset by limiting space in order to be able to create it. (The window or the transparent wall is, in reality, a direct connection to the outside and destroys the impression of space. Therefore it should be used with great discretion; only where a definite function exists.) It is now, a question of making the most of this space enclosed by translucent glass blocks. The dynamism of the fourth dimension in contrast to the static. The static in architecture is the structure supporting that which should be perpetually fixed. Completely independent of this is the dynamic expressed by the horizontal and vertical distribution, by the fixed and moving partitions, by the built-in furniture and by the staircases, etc. The columns are coordinates, which, regularly spaced, establish points around which the functional layout is irregularly organized.

The Chareau House is not immobile nor is it photographic; it is cinematographic. One must pass through the spaces in order to be able to appreciate it; another aspect by which it is connected to contemporary man.

It is built. It functions. It is not solely based on the dictates of abstract ideas, for it works. The walls are solid; the

sliding doors slide. There are no leaks. The air conditioning works. It would appear that one does not suffer from
either the heat or the cold. It is realized.

This house is a point of departure. Herein technical problems have been tackled and bravely resolved up to the
last detail. Pure aesthetic research has not been the aim
here, but strangely enough, solely through technical
research, this house has outstripped surrealist sculpture.
Calder and Giacometti would be able to see its realization in these terms. The pivoting door suspended in front
of the main stairway is a surrealist sculpture of great
Beauty. The metal cupboards are similarly so. All this has
been achieved without having any desire to make art for
art's sake.

"Modern architecture" is dying. It has become a romanti-
cism, a sentimentalism best expressed in literature and
in music. Now a technological architecture emerges, a
realizable architecture wholly conditioned by the requirements of the new life and by a real knowledge of building.
Chareau knew how to limit himself. It is because of this
that he has created a beautiful work, which one recog-
nizes as a point of departure towards a true architecture.

*From L'Architecture d'Aujourd'hui, No. 9, November/
December 1933, p. 9.

在实践中的领导/团队合作, 第2部分
对**Helle Søholt** 和 **Olafur Eliasson**的采访

Peter MacKeith

彼得•马克吉斯

彼得•马克吉斯（Peter MacKeith）奥拉维尔•埃利亚松工作室和盖尔建筑师事务行作为富有艺术性的设计实践各有一个很有力和简单的标志性的公司名字—一个标示个人名称的公司名字—同时也被认为注重于团队精神和协作的跨学科实践。您可以描述出你们公司最初形成的过程，包括公司的名字吗？是否从一开始就存在一种合作方式，或至少拥有跨学科的思维？

赫勒•索荷特（Helle Søholt）当然可以。我们公司创立开始就采用了合作的方式。有一点必须要记住的是在公司形成的时候，杨•盖尔六十四岁而我才二十八岁。这年龄上的差异曾引起了许多有关如何合作共同建立公司的讨论。虽然从开始我们就知道公司将注重于杨•盖尔对于中心城区的概念 - "交往与空间" - 当我们也知道这不会是一个人的公司。当然，我们选择的公司名是用复数表现 - 盖尔建筑师事务行—城市品质顾问咨询公司 - 就是共同发展规划和设计最好的证明。在这同时，我们想如果我们够成功的话，公司的寿命将能超越我们。我的志向是在这些合作方式的基础上建立一个团队。而且，事实上，不同于个别的建筑师，杨从未在图纸上签署他的名字，不管他是不是这项设计工作的领导。

就算我和杨之间有着年龄上的差距，我们一直都视自己为"年轻"的公司，或者更直接一点说是现代化的公司。现代化的定义是我们很清楚大部分员工以及其他合作人士的相对年龄。更具体一点说的话就是我们现在是在Y世代的世界里工作，而Y世代则是希望能够在自己的设计角色中拥有更多的参与感和更多的控制。

至于我们公司的起源，杨在开始的时候就已经在城市设计研究学术界拥有40年的职业生涯，也是哥本哈根皇家学院城市设计研究组的领导。我的志愿是将这些研究应用到现实中。所以正如杨在研究组中的工作，所有的项目都是从对该城市条件进行谨慎和深入的研究开始。从而，我们能

一方面不断地保持学术性研究而另一方面又能将研究成功地转移到现实城市生活中。我们将继续发展我们的方法、工具以及我称之为我们设计领导的方法。

但是在整个发展中，我们依然保持了原先的精神 "交往与空间" - 也就是将重点放在了居住在城市中的市民。其实也可以说是 "盖尔"标示着 "人们的设计" ... 这是我们的品牌，超越了一个人。盖尔建筑师事务行已变成 "设计人们"以及在城市设计中采用可持续方式的代名词。

奥拉维尔•埃利亚松（Olafur Eliasson）工作室的源头是希望能创造艺术。如果某个项目需要专门的技能，那么我们就会找合适的人选去做。我们工作室引进了众多专业技能的人士，渐渐扩大到包括技术高超的工匠、艺术处理师、电影工作者、训练有素的建筑师和工程师、程序员、档案保管员、艺术史学家、厨师及几何学家。而工作室的组成则反映出所有我们创造的艺术品和展览。很多核心人员从公司最早开始的时候就跟我一起工作了，不过工作室的界限还是相对的开放，一直保持着人来人往。有些为我工作的人也会为其他人或者自己工作。

比如说，一个特别复杂的项目 - 如Harpa雷克雅未克音乐厅和会议中心的立面设计 - 就会需要一个内部建筑师团队。这个团队由塞巴斯蒂安•贝曼（Sebastian Behmann）负责，我从2001年开始就跟他合作。另一位和我也是长期的合作者，埃纳尔•索尔斯泰恩（Einar Thorsteinn）则开发了准砖背后用于建造立面模块的几何。我和塞巴斯蒂安在各种建筑项目上也会和若干人等合作，从复杂的几何形态到像在乌克兰第聂伯彼得罗夫斯克Interpipe工厂的Double Sunrise 这种大规模工程或者像位于哥本哈根的Cirkelbroen桥。

相似的，档案相对于传统意义上被动的存档，其实在我们来说是较为积极的实体并涉及到知识的生产。在开发这种方式的同时，我们的档案将继续增长并扩展到新的领域，

如社交媒体、出版物和电影制作。它已经渐渐成为独立的个体,或许称之为档案是种误导。

总的来说,我希望我团队的所有人都能对工作拥有非常强烈的共同责任感。虽然我还是保留了对关键艺术元素的抉择权,但还是希望在有一天能把某些决定交给其他人。如果要实现这种想法,他们必须理解工作背后的原则。当大家对于工作的要点更为敏感的时候,他们就会变得更自主。如果我能将大家充分的融入到工作中,那他们的工作表现也相反的能激励到我。

PM:随着许多不同的成就记录,盖尔建筑事务行在设计文化中有了一席之地。埃利亚松工作室也伴随着许多的成就在不同的领域和区域上包括艺术、建筑和设计文化也占有一席之地。如果不考虑作品以及聘用的设计师,合作者和助手,您认为归因于埃利亚松和盖尔名字吗? 当公司成长和吸引越来越多不同的项目时,这些价值是如何跨越了不同的设计师、作品、地点.....而保持一致的?

HS:我们和普通建筑公司的区别在于我们是跟整个城市合作,包括当代城市所面临的挑战和复杂性,如密集化、住宅、基础设施等。我们需要同时顾及现有城市的质量以及新发展的压力。当你要为这些重要的问题特别是城市中市民的生活质量提供咨询时,我们相信这必须是一个需要通过协作的过程。我们的基本原则是共同创造:和城市合作、与领导人合作、持续的讨论和评估。我们和城市及领导合作创建可持续城市设计,然后教导他们根据自己的条件来解决这些复杂的问题。

我们在过去五年的工作中涉及到五十七座城市。世界各地对于城市设计质量一直不断的增长。当我们的雄心不在于项目的数量或者大小,而是出于对能力建设、授权和思想领导的愿景。我的意思是希望凭借我们的研究和经验给出的支持和建议,各城市能够了解自己并做出决策。套用一句名言,我们是教人钓鱼,而不是给人鱼。公司在很多方面都是从根本上的合作及参与,会在聘用我们的城市中举办讲座、会议、研讨会和设计审核。通过这种方式,所有的人 — 利益相关者以及市民 — 都拥有权力决定自己城市的未来。

我之前就提到过我们是一个年轻和现代化的公司,同时又依赖团队合作。如果要达到可信以及成功的团队合作,每一位员工都须拥有以下三种特质:1)适用于不同文化的领导能力,也就是他必须对工作的集体知识和实践有足够的自信、意识到盖尔研究的深度以及能在不同环境中传递这些知识;2)关心(不是骄傲),能够充当一个聆听者

并拥有文化意识,参与不同兴趣和抱负的讨论、利用盖尔"工具箱"中策略和分析达到针对个别城市的创新解决方案;3)乐观,必须相信你能创建更好的地方。我们真诚地相信即使在最坏的地方也有机会创造出好的东西。我需要补充的是这三个特质不是能够教出来的,因此我们对未来员工的面试过程是非常透彻和深入的。

我的领导方式是给于意见和建议但须永远强调协作性。我们是一家知识公司,所以彼此之间分享知识是非常重要的。我们平日会花很多时间讨论项目和方案因为在与各城市、时区和地区的团队合作的时候都必须要保持信息统一。我们会利用几种方式来实现这种一致性的内部信息。例如,一年四次我们会举行所谓的"知识日"...这几天我们公司会关门,大家选出一个主题,然后通过讨论来达到对这个主题的共识。还有我们每周都会举行午餐汇报来向互相报告工作。我能说的是我们会持续地进行讨论,同意知识中永远不止一种解决方案并推进建立可持续城市文化的新途径。我们经常说无论是公司内部还是与城市及市民一起的工作都是学习多于决定。

OE:这跟维持一定的审美或属性无关,而是我们如何解决一组问题的方法 – 共同创造空间、移位、责任和感知。我本人以及我的工作室通过这种媒体和情况来探讨这些问题。这反而更能明确问题和可能的解决方案(思考,实行,思考,实行...)。这有可能是跟创造空间的问题有关 – 无论是公共、建筑或其他 – 或是有关同情、与他人相处、也或者是个人或团体经历的问题。在这个意义上,我认为工作应该是种实验的设置而不是静态的研究对象。

至于有关合作的问题,我希望能强调的是一件艺术品只要遇到观众就会形成一种合作。艺术品在离开工作室进入它本身的环境后就会产生意义,无论是通过观众还是它被展示或运用的环境。

PM:您会如何描述埃利亚松工作室或盖尔建筑事务所的工作方式,或者对团队合作概念的理解? 与个人作为设计者的平行发展的思想相关,或者甚至是 "设计的领导地位,"团队合作在盖尔的典型项目的概念化和实现中起到了什么样的作用? 如果这是一个中心价值或方法,如何鼓励,培养或者加强?有哪些方法去鼓励强调这种方法? 但是否也有缺点?

HS:我所描述的知识分享方式本身就具有挑战性,主要是因为我们都在知识共享的分级制度中成长 – 一直都是由一位老师教导一群学生。对于公司和我们的合作伙伴来说,问题是如何将个人的知识和经验变得组织化以及集体的经

验。事实上，拥有许多参与者的知识共享过程很有可能会导致决策时间变得缓慢。但是如果将它与所获得的知识深度和绝对的质量之间做对比，我们认为这是非常值得的。

除了集合知识分享较慢以外，还需考虑专业关系大多数也是较为私人得 ...客户已习惯于顾问保持私人和个人的关系。但是我们最好的作品其实是那些能够理解我们团队工作方式得城市领导 - 因为他必须知道我们一直都是选用对该项目过程最适合得人选。这种方式可能在现在这种由客户经理去维持客户关系常规的实践中存在着异议。但从我们的角度上来看，城市设计属复杂的过程而我们的每位团员都能够按照个人专长解决对应的问题，如住宅、数据收集、勘测方法和基础设施研究。也就是说每位团员都能按照自己的专长在工作过程中成为适当和必须的盖尔代表。这就是所谓的智慧共享及以团队为基础的顾问。这里存在着双重标准：客户必须信任我们的方法而我们的团队则需要提供一致的专业性和高质量的交付成果。

如我先前所说，我们和普通传统的公司不同的地方在于我们的专业是城市。而城市又在工作中需要自身特殊的特征。我们做的工作最终会变成变成它的工作。作为顾问，我们需要给于支撑，有时会得到认证有时又没。简单来说，我们给城市提供建议但最终的功劳依然归功于城市。当我们和市民、社会团队和领导合作的时候，这个最终功劳是非常明确的。跟城市领导者相比，我们较常会与希望得到功劳的建筑师发生冲突。因此我们会寻找能理解这个道理的合作者合作。

OE：我觉得现在大众在判断一件艺术品成功与否最主要的标准是所谓的精确度。很多人都会觉得成功和精确度在一方面代表着艺术家原本的想法而另一方面又直接就是完成品。对我来说，最重要的应该是团队如何精确的将想法完完全全的演变成一件完成的艺术品。团队合作的实际过程、精确的同步性以及运行轨迹跟成功之间有莫大关联。当你要创造一件成品时，这种将想法转变成一件艺术品的方式正是它成功以及精确的关键。这就是呈现精密度的方式。

我们整个工作室结构的存在是协作从构想变成现实的过程，帮助创造新的现实。当然有一帮值得信赖的同僚一起分享和讨论我的构想过程是很有帮助的 - 是因我比较喜欢在团队中工作 - 但这存在于更深的意义：我一个人去判断一件东西的潜力其实还是比较困难。每件物品都是社会构造的，也就是说它们的意义往往在人群中才得以实现。我个人在看一件事物的时候可能会觉得毫无灵感但如果是跟其他人一起的话或许就能对它产生兴趣，然后得出更好的想法。从某种意义上来说，我是通过其他人的存在去看事物的。

还有当我和其他人一起工作的时候，我会感到更强烈的暂时性，时间会流失得更快。这种对时间的意识使得我对工作更加的积极。跟单独工作相比，我跟团队一起合作的时候工作会更有效率。

PM：您也担任过教职并教导过实习生，帮组他们为专业实践做准备。如何将团队和合作的概念（在重申一次，相对于个人创作和设计领导）带进您与学生间的讨论？ 这样的方法和态度是能通过教导的方式传送给学生吗？ 如果能的话，又如何做到呢？

HS：设计学校中有许多巨大挑战。我们希望有创意的思想家和带领团队领导者都能进入设计领域中。建筑师，特别是城市设计师，正成为设计改革的促进者 - 但这角色最能实现的是合作的创造者。再一次重申，这些倾向于协作和知识共享的特质并不能在教室中学习到，但同样的也没有教程是能够教导这些的。我认为学生在学时期的时候更应接触到"现实生活，"特别是在社会活动这一块，例如参加本地政府活动等。确实有些学校是有界限的理想地方：思想和知识准备的"自由区 。"这种理想的大学校区对于设计师的发展是非常重要的。但我同时又认为好的学生设计师必须能对真正的流程、现实的情况以及实用的解决方案产生意识。我相信学生是能够和应该学习一定程度上的实用主义因为这个世界并不完美而我们的工具箱中是需要结合乐观和实用主义才能有效地展开工作。

我们相信我们能做出示例性的项目，但须藉由对不同观点的平衡。

OE：我必须要提到我在教学也是和两位同事一起合作，分别是埃里克•艾林森（Eric Ellingsen）和克里斯蒂娜•维尔纳（Christina Werner）。两位都深入参与到 Raumexperimente研究所各种事项中，包括筹办讨论、试验、展览、出版和竞走活动。

虽然大部分教学是群体制，不过很令人惊讶的是人们往往会忽视其实处于群组中的经验比教师要传达的信息更有教育意义。虽然我并不完全主动地鼓励学生团体合作，但我觉得通过和别人分享想法、沟通或甚于简单到只处在人群中都能学习到东西。我常常发现很多学生从团队活动中通过实现自己的想法或者互相沟通的时候会学习到更多。所以您也可以说，教学本身对我来说就是一个非常要求团队协作的过程而老师也只是这过程中其中的一位而已。

Agency and Authorship
机构和作者
An Interview with John Harwood
对John Harwood的采访

Peter MacKeith

彼得•马克吉斯

Peter MacKeith: 彼得. 马克吉斯：在最近发表与政治经济学家乔纳森. 莱维的探讨中，您提出"以资本作为主体"的概念作为与建筑特定相关问题。"自上世纪十九年代末期以来，在依照企业管理和金融咨询公司建筑业公司如viz., Arup, SOM － 等的模式运营下，建筑业公司凭借自身实力转型为拥有成百上千客户的巨大企业。"我很欣赏您就这点而言的想法（调解，代表性，抽象化），可是您能否对此思维加以扩展 － 这一转型对当代建筑作品发展过程中理想与现实之间的影响以及设计决策的过程？自第二次世界大战之后这种专业实践的转型已初现倪端，但并得不到大众或众多建筑历史学家的充分认识。"领导者"与"作者"的思想理念在这次转型中如何体现？

John Harwood: 约翰.哈伍德：就我理解，您是指决策分析管理秘诀的持久性问题。也就是说在任何理性的角度来看独立个体应为决策者。长久以来打破此观点的不仅仅是人类学家、哲学家和理论家们，也包括创造我们现代生活中的巨大即兴综合体如跨国公司、政府机构、网络和市场的资本家，经济学家以及科学家们。"网络"和"市场"掌握了整个社会生活体系与与时代不符的（强）作者。个人 － 通常是"个体"的一种生物政治缩写 － 确实会做出不同决策，比如早餐土司上要什么配料，当不能还款信用卡公司时该如何应对等问题。然而这些平凡的决策却高度受限：一块土司的可配种类是有限的，您必须有钱去购买想要的配料，必须有公司生产并推广这些配料等等。这些约束条件都是科技性，经济性和社会性的产物。

同样清楚的是，当个体作为"决策者"或"领导人"，甚至作为首席执行官或国家元首，他或她做任何决策的能力也受到同样甚至更多的限制。那些做过领导位置的人都明白这一点。从这个角度看，人们可能会带些许同情去评判冷战期间总统或掌握着众所周知的红按钮的将军、或商人在解雇工人还是与投资者共同承担损失中作出的选择，即便是在工人受到大多数人同情的情况下。换而言之，自亚当•斯密以来，或者至少自如博弈论和运筹学等理论管理工具的出现以来，应该再没有任何以个人行为为核心数据集的历史出现过。这不是历史而是一种社会变迁史。这当然也是在更深入权力性质的争论上涂上一层粗燥的表面而已。

有人也许会用"代理"这个比喻词的角度上来看待这个问题。当作为代理人即表示此人拥有代理权，便倾向于驳倒所有证明"权力凌驾于现实"的证据。然而作为代理却恰恰相反。公民是国家的代理；保险经纪是保险集团的服务者；旅游中介是以公司名义为他人制定旅行计划。一个人愿意与否去完成指派的任务并不重要，关键是去完成它。

因此就我认为，在所有建筑师和历史学家中存在一个深刻的问题。很明显，虽然每个人的行为都是自身的抉择并也只是对做此抉择的人具有意义，但他并不能单靠自己制定设计或历史叙事需要的原始数据。更糟的是，从已存在的设计问题或历史叙述的角度来看的话，原本觉得至关重要的个人抉择其实到头来变得无关紧要。在这些情况下抉择本身就该被视为不足以引起任何事情的缘由，因为在错综复杂的因果关系网里它并不能影响设计师作出更大型的设计方案或成为历史学家看待历史事件的原因。

作为建筑历史学家，我以全新的角度来考虑这个问题后

而做出微乎其微的个人意见中，我一直着重简单倒置法的影响。暂时将个人决定的评估放在一边（虽然以后这些在细节讨论中会非常有用），而首先去试图描述企业的整体情况，我们可以先回避整个问题的根源（至少暂时的，因为语法和某些言语段落总能把我们拉回原先的错误观点），然后将复杂的历史事件看成是因综合体与人类生活群体的相互作用（而非抉择）的产物。毕竟，如果不是上层建筑最初的建立以及不断的改建（在真正的虚构意义上）令人类能够作为合作群体而不是作为一群单独的个体存在，又何来企业的存在？

我和很多当代的历史学家所追溯的建筑作品创造者的转变无疑自二次世界大战后加快了进程；可是，应该辩证地看待这种转型，在此漫漫长路中我们可以追溯到自中世纪末期。在被称之为高级或全球化的资本主义时期里，我们可以看到：简单地看待建筑品的创造者是不足够去描述我们所处的世界的，这其实促使我们去探究一个非常被意大利文艺复兴时期的艺术家，艺术评论家和学者们所熟识的问题。

PM: SOM8 和9中将希区柯克（Hitchcock）的文章《The Architecture of Bureaucracy and the Architecture of Genius》作其背景参考。此书也不久前在《Hunch》得到再版并得到琼．奥卡姆（Joan Ockman）热情洋溢的介绍。在即将出版的《Perspecta》中您也对这篇文章做出了非常详细的研究。我认为他的论述非常带有当代性。他所推崇解决矛盾的方法在当今看来依旧适用 – 以一种更为微妙（甚至是隐伏的）的方式。如果我理解正确的话，硅谷总部实际上在"透明度、灵活性和趣味性"的面具背后隐藏了其"官僚主义"的运作方式，并且通过"天才"设计的这种艺术性表现来论证其"企业"特征。希区柯克是否因经济、科技和文化的剧烈变迁而需要更新他的观点？ 在这样的回顾上再加以评论的重点又是什么？

JH: 我绝对赞同您对希区柯克文章有着来世不朽的魅力的评价，而且我也认同其具有深刻的当代意义。我在《Perspecta》的文章中试图解释为什么希区柯克的文章

和另一篇来自上世纪40年代约翰． 萨默森（John Summerson）的"The Mischievous Analogy"文章仍然困扰我们这些在建筑文化中的人。我们理解建筑师和建筑历史学家在了解企业以及其对当代建筑实践的重要性时所面对的差距和问题。简而言之，我的观点是这样的：

二战结束时，建筑历史学家已停止谈论企业的性质及其对建筑生产的影响等此类问题。甚至如Manfredo Tafuri那些公认最致力于唯物主义观点的历史学家，即认为建筑是基本经济条件下产生的上层建筑，也没有或许无法解决这个关键问题。而希区柯克于1947年在《建筑评论》中发布的的文章则成为了"最后的定论"，尽管文章当中极具推测和折射性。他相信他看到的事情，因此推测，建筑产业的变革而且很可能会威胁到建筑设计的品质，传统的建筑实践已经或者将来会分为三个完全不同的建筑活动模式：为大规模企业设计建筑的传统建筑师（或小规模公司）；拥有跨国公司运行模式的新兴建筑公司（希区柯克引用了阿尔伯特·卡恩公司和SOM为例）；以及有可能但不是既定事实和带有神秘性的"天才建筑"。这些分类及与它们相关的条款在细微的调整后至今仍被运用。特别是比如说在建筑学校里二十世纪建筑的课程中，继有关科比意（Le Corbusier）的三节课后，学生就只需要参加一节合并二战前工厂建筑、装饰艺术和二战后办公楼建筑以及一些TAC的建筑物的课。对于很多学生来说二战的课最多只是分隔有关柯布的课程而已。

在我看来，我们必须注意到希区柯克是旨在通过吸引不能单靠一个无形的企业结构来进行各种独特和个人风格设计而去拯救那些过时的独立创造者的观点。不用说，希区柯克认为其模范天才是弗兰克·劳埃德·赖特（Frank Lloyd Wright），认为他像一个"有机"解围人，能够解救企业设计试图将建筑的艺术性完全挤掉的危机。但从希区柯克选择在文章中附有古根海姆未完成的设计图片中能看一点，也许他并没有在第一次阅读天才的胜利时听起来那么的自信。

PM：你著作的《The Interface》中以及其它在现代建筑历史中工作的人都很明显的强调现代文化中信息与数字

科技的存储与发展及其转型的影响，并体现在建筑环境与建筑实践中。在《The Interface》中，您提到IBM是自身接合企业特征的代表案例，其基础不仅存在于与科技的认识而在于科技的发展潜力和影响。其他研究当代实践表示这些科技现今已改变了建筑实践的传统阶级概念 — "著作权"，"所有权"和"知识"。您如果同意我的评价的话，请问是否能够举出在当代建筑实践中被认可的实例，一个基于技术发展潜力而成为更加清晰和高效的公司？或者您有其他能参考的实践模型 — 这些科技实际上是否能真的使得公司远离企业模式？

JH：我是一位历史学家，所以我对当代的批评，预测和未来学感到不安。确实现在很多人关心某些科技对当今建筑实践基本条件的影响的根本性和紧迫的问题。既然所有的历史都以这样或那样的方式与当今汇合，我当然也关心同样的问题。

为了不要看起来过份谨慎小心，也许我能够以这种方式回答你的问题：我相信我们所见，包括那些在当代建筑实践中运用电脑科技的我们所不能看到的。在全方位电脑化的当今时代，可以保证的是至少在当下建筑文化中很多方面还会持续发展。一方面就是建筑学院加速电脑科技及其外围设备用于基本实践应用和市场研究。曾经是由跨国高科技公司出资赞助麻省理工学院的少数精品和密环的运行模式现今几已运用在每个雄心勃勃的建筑学院；只要给予我们基本配备，我们就能对其改装再以成果展示出我们的能力。我不打算任何方式去对这种状况加以评估（虽然我确实希望师生们能给予其他重要建筑类活动相同甚至更多的支持与重视），但是我认为这是一个一直被重复的议题。

另外一个是持续运用表面作为当代建筑实践的主要调节概念（而在这点上建筑师绝对不是唯一的）。我们已从上世纪50-60年代视面板和图形界面为电脑工业设计的主要创新，虽然仍无法理解，转至无论任何知识都必须是表现在作品上。（我特别尊崇地质学家与建筑师约翰.梅（John May）对这一主题的研究）这不仅延伸至将电脑界面降低为华丽界面的概念，是建筑师通过阅读，操控及创造作品时思考的表现。虽然我们也许不该忽视那些处理成本计算、结构模拟和物流的软件，但现在已作为建筑设计的这些易操作的主要工具，如GIS，IBM当然也包括3D模型和制作应用等等（这一点我支持帕诺夫斯基的观点，没有什么绝对的二维模式），能够保证建筑作品的最终品质。

最后，我们现在处在一种无法从建筑创作中避免企业性质的阶段，虽然我们至今仍无法接受这个事实。就我看来，今天去想象任何建筑师或建筑历史学家能够不按照

企业的约束去创造自己的作品是几乎没有意义的。不偏执的人也能够充分的理解这一点。今天的我们周围一切都被企业所包围：包括州（美国国家有多少州，又分市政、郡县、州和联邦不同级别），自愿组织、专业组织、学校、企业等。

谈到你所询问的科技问题，既然这都是以及永远都会是由企业来生产和分布的，所以这不是为企业所用就是被企业所控制。这就无法避免将用户引导至更深的企业组织模式。我同意莱因霍尔德.马丁（Reinhold Martin）的观点，如今对于这种情况没有例外。企业条件是建筑的绝对本质，这不单单存在于资本主义，而作为轮廓来看，知识的主体在成为其本身之前先发展为科技和社会。每当我忽略这一点的时候，就会翻看维特鲁威的第二部著作第一章和他关于此专业的观点。一道闪电划过大树-转化为能量，普罗米修斯手握火焰降落至凡间大地。这一点就莫里斯.希基.摩根的话描述为："（愤怒的火焰）消退之后，他们日益临近，可看出他们非常舒适地站在温暖的火堆之前，添柴以维持火种，并在更多前来的人们面前用手语表达他们的舒适感。这就是在人类社会火的起源，由此带来一系列协商讨论以及社会交往。"接下来就是模拟学院和避难所。科技，语言，社交，企业组织，构架这些整体结构和次序是简单但不能被逆转。

暂时回到20世纪中期，我总结两个简短的轶事。在1940年出版哈罗德•范多伦关于仍然相对年轻的工业设计实践的书中，通过运用一些卡通并令人信服的图像-他阐述了能够在为企业客户（他称它们为"公司"）在设计的作品上能够保留一点自主权的唯一途径不是加入企业，而是成为企业内在。如果设计师积极面对公司的各方各面，而不只充当企业层的某个角落的一个小角色，这样设计师机构发展是广阔和富有建设性的。我认为在当今仍然值得考虑这个建议。

最后，是SOM的创始合伙人和第一位"催化剂" — 纳撒尼尔•奥因斯（Nathaniel Owings），他通过观察自己的企业在回忆录中写道："我们成为了什么？我们肯定不能回答自己是经典意义上的设计师。我们可以是企业家，推动者，稽查员，金融家，外交官；我们涉及许多行业当不是任何一个的大师。"我想在今天对于没有受到怀旧或遗憾情感影响而接受建筑业人士已从根本上做出改变的人来说，那么设想一种更好的建筑企业实践模式可能会更为简单一些。

Gordon Bunshaft: What Convinces Is Conviction
戈登•邦夏：具有说服力的领导者

Nicholas Adams
尼古拉斯•亚当斯

"如我们一样的平凡人" [1]

很少有建筑师能像戈登•邦夏（Gordon Bunshaft: 1909–1990）这样偶然地走进这个行业：读书、旅行、二战前入职。退役后他回到工作岗位，这家公司在他缺席期间就已成规模发展，证明其有实力承接政府大型建筑工程项目。他的设计执着于实现设计愿景，给自己设定了严苛的标准，老板们也因此愿意给他足够的设计自由。剩下的只是历史，还是戈登•邦夏的职业道路成为人们可以适应时代、展示新形势下不同领导模式的典范?

当然是戈登•邦夏所生活和工作的时代造就了他。他的行为举止像个行业巨人、果敢决断的军中将军、建筑业的约翰•韦恩（John Wayne）。认识他的人们还清楚记得他的不拘礼数、沉默寡言、断续的三段论理论。[2] 邦夏的意见总是简洁精练。他提出合理解决方案；发现的是需要规划的缺失部分；决定的是客户想要的东西；或至少是，按照客户当前理解所需要的东西。然后他就不再多说什么了。这是时代的偶然性：SOM有爱出风头的推销员，现代建筑的不言而喻：邦夏保持了沉默。十多年来，建筑风格的确是人人想要的。1960年以前，戈登•邦夏是SOM的唯一一名设计合伙人。

戈登•邦夏以其开发的利华大厦（1952）、汉华实业银行大厦（1954）、大通银行（1961）建筑外立面和框架以及开发新型混凝土建筑而声名鹊起。他倾听、提问和学习。他还是不拘礼数，甚至偶尔有些粗鲁，习惯性的沉默，以同样简捷的方式回应问题：这必须得做；这是合乎逻辑的解决方案；这样的回答让人无法拒绝。尽管他不再是SOM唯一的设计合伙人，而且常常会被其他合伙人轻视，但邦夏还是公认的领导人。他开玩笑地说，他的名字之所以没有放在公司名头上，因为如果那样的话，公司的名字就成了"S.O.B.（骂人粗语）"。[3]

在二十世纪七十年代，在困难重重的逆境中，邦夏还是那个邦夏，一个说得少、写得少，以简短回答表达个人

判断，像个后卫一样与后现代主义保持着距离。[4] 他还是把问题推出身外，让它们自生自灭。当他在SOM职业生涯即将结束的时候，有些人认为呆得太久会不受欢迎，邦夏却还是迎难而上，与年轻雇员合作，推出广受赞誉的原创作品。之后，他离开了——1979年退休，年之后去世。

除了他的建筑作品，邦夏没留下什么值得关注的东西。他手上有些图纸，大部分来自他的学生时代，仅有几个可见他考虑问题思路的备选方案，没有文章或讲稿，尚存的访谈记录着他那令人熟悉的断续的三段论理论。他位于纽约长岛（1963）的房子于2008年被拆除，关于他个人生活的最后线索也无从考察了，现代艺术博物馆已将他捐赠的大部分艺术收藏品分散出去。他的家庭（无子女）不愿公开谈论这个复杂的男人。所以了解他如何身处高位——评估他对于从未加他名字的公司意味着什么——我们只有找到那些认识邦夏作为公众人物的人们，并研究他留下的往来信件。

与时代的必然关联。当他二战后返回SOM时，在现代艺术博物馆的推动下，在得到富有赞助人的支持、出版物的倡导、渴望摆脱战前方式的一代人的推崇下，围绕现代建筑文化品位已开始形成。所以一家能将新鲜事物做成生意的公司本身就有新闻价值。1958年《财富杂志》报道的"Skid's Boys"据称体现的是战胜德国人和日本人的某种无私的团队合作；一个没有个人意志的工作室，完全代表的是客户和国家的意愿，每个员工都是威廉•怀特（William H. Whyte）"组织人" [5] 的完美示范。事实上，SOM没有公布设计师的名字，而是以"委员会设计"或"大会设计"的形式推广自己，使公司文化体现在对建筑的思考，提升团体的社会道德标准 [6]。在当代艺术博物馆1950年展览目录中，博物馆首次专门展示SOM一家公司（而非建筑师个人）作品的殊荣——SOM的成绩得益于两个专业："现代建筑"以及"美国团队组织方法"。[7] 邦夏二战回归时一定赞同这样的方式。但是十多年后，就在《财富杂志》文章刊登之后，邦夏开

始被激怒了。在一年之后的《新闻周刊》中，邦夏否认了所谓的"由委员会设计"的说法，"应该总有主导的某个人提出原创设计"。后来在同一文章中，他提出："我是项目的负责人。其他合伙人也参与了设计，但通过批判的方式"。[8] 其他合伙人对此评论提出指责。

尽管如此，他仍然是不可缺少的人物，"合伙人们希望他留下，或是他们需要他。"由于他善于适应时代要求，他们允许邦夏为整个公司的设计建立统一标准。他做得很好。英国建筑师约翰•温特（John Winter）（生于1930年）介绍说他在1958年旧金山办公室见到邦夏。温特当时几个星期都在解决一个难解的问题（美国银行，萨克拉门托），"听说伟大的戈登•邦夏正在从纽约办公室赶过来。消息很快传遍整个办公室，我们当时都很兴奋。我只是把他想像成一个强硬的生意人，而他的到来却让人印象深刻。我给他看了我的萨克拉门托项目并说出了那个问题。他拿出铅笔，用了30秒的时间涂鸦了几笔，所有问题就都解决了"。[9] 正如他的高级设计师罗杰•雷德福（Roger Radford: SOM 1953–90）所说："...我认为邦夏在纽约发挥的是领导力...也就是实际上所有的建筑...成果都有他的印记"。[10] 在邦夏宣称为他自己设计的38座建筑清单中，他的影响或介入是不容置疑的：正像邦夏就在那里。[11]

他的影响表现在对于全国各地其它办公室设计的介入。[12] 有些众所周知，例如内陆钢铁大厦（芝加哥，1957年）或空军学院（科泉市，1958年）；有些较少人知晓，如老兵纪念体育馆（波特兰，1957年）。其全有些建筑没有证据证明他给出过意见，比如泽勒巴赫皇冠公司大厦（Crown Zellerbach Building:旧金山，1959年），取决于邦夏——就是说在SOM，他被公认为民间风格的创始人，不是纯真或未经训练的，不是现代主义者，而是在整个公司范围内的。1960年，《建筑论坛》刊登一篇文章说明原型SOM细节。题为"区别的细节"，文章记录了邦夏重要建筑的吊顶、窗墙及门框：美国联合碳化物公司、康涅狄格通用人寿保险公司总部、汉华实业银行大厦、利华大厦、雷诺兹金属公司。文章还包括了一直由邦夏而是由其同事提供重要影响的建筑：内陆钢铁大厦（芝加哥，沃尔特•纳什，布鲁斯•格雷厄姆，1957年）、哈特福特火灾保险大厦（芝加哥，布鲁斯•格雷厄姆及娜塔莉，1961年），沃伦石油公司行政总部大楼（布鲁斯•格雷厄姆，1957年）。"从这些细节研究来看"，作者写道："最终形成了出奇制胜的建筑设计——除了似乎浑然天成的完美之处。"[13] 其中有摄影大师Ezra Stoller（埃兹拉.斯托勒）拍摄邦夏建筑作品而值得其他合伙人借鉴的独特摄影风格，这样的摄影手法令建筑看似相似，而并非一模一样。

邦夏于二十世纪五十年代声名大噪（甚至令他服务的公司相形见绌），第二个和第三个十年见证了他的改变能力，这是他早年职场和个性所始料不及的。

新的建筑发展趋势被引入当时的社会[14] 1954年4月，邦夏提出未来建筑的发展趋势："我们为什么要急着摈弃矩形建筑呢？我们为什么不设计几个优秀建筑呢？"[15] 不到四年后，1958年1月，欧文士（Nathaniel Owings）在访谈中明确表示："公司并非一定要做'不锈钢标准'，这是市场竞争的要求。我们感兴趣的是可塑性，我们正在探索各种途径实现这一目标。"[16] 无论是建筑师密斯的西格拉姆大厦（Seagram Building）、勒•柯布西耶的朗香教堂（Ronchamp）和昌迪加尔市（Chandigarh）城市规划，还是布鲁斯•格雷厄姆和 沃尔特•纳什在芝加哥以及查克-巴西特在旧金山的成熟设计作品——遍地开花。追求变化需要这位粗暴大师的回应。与保罗•威林格（Paul Weidlinger: 1914–1999）合作的几年不仅产生了新型建筑，还令邦夏有了全新的改变。莱昂（SOM 1954–91）回忆称这种形式的合作与邦夏的本性不符。而势在必行的改变使他必须接受挑战。他对于幕墙技术一清二楚。他可能到处要求这样做，但不大清楚哪些可行、哪些不可行。而混凝土是另一回事。在二十世纪五十年代，邦夏在设计顺利推进之前，推迟了与工程师的大量研讨，而与威林格的合作，他表达了希望初期研讨的意愿："我们知道混凝土可以做各种东西...但我们需要学习。一旦我们有了初步想法，高级设计师、保罗和我——主要是保罗和我——将碰头讨论。保罗有时会说"你不能这样做"，但他却从来不提出设计建议。"[17] 二十世纪六十年代晚期，与邦夏合作密切的莱昂表示威林格是个"真正的合作者"，这是决断的邦夏此前所不曾需要的。

邦夏有能力将这样的变化掌控为风格——不仅是建筑风格，也是确保他在SOM领导地位的做事风格。他随着时代在改变。在康涅狄格州布卢姆菲尔德的埃姆哈特公司（1963年）和纽黑文市善本图书馆（1963年）项目上几乎瞬间的成功让邦夏证明他不仅是个工具。他虽然不再是SOM首席设计师，也不再是领导此建筑风格，但他还能够以领导的方式行事。他可以分配资源。1963年，当旧金山办公室希望与戴维斯•艾伦（Davis Allen）合作莫纳克亚山度假区（1965年）的室内设计时，他们征询了SOM纽约办公室主管威廉斯•布朗（William S. Brown）的意见。在他同意的基础上，他们又征求戈登•邦夏关于由戴维斯•艾伦参与项目的许可。[18] 艾伦随后将他（和邦夏）设法插入大通银行（1961年）的部分审美设计用到了莫纳克亚山度假区项目，成为似是而非的邦夏风格。戴维斯•艾伦的普遍性的确成为邦夏品味及风格[19]的另一种表现。读了芝加哥办公室《室内设计》（1959年1月）期刊中的一篇文章后，有人或许会问，文章提出的是否真的是独特的"芝加哥"室内设计风格。[20]

而重要的是，不要把邦夏性格刻画得过于宽泛。邦夏通常只是太忙而难抓到他人：角落办公室里的决策人物，带着强烈信念而可能对同事苛刻的人。一次，他让娜塔莉回家换衣服（他不喜欢绿色——难道不是每个人都知道SOM不用绿色的吗？）；对于他不想说话的人他会不予理睬——无论是合伙人还是合伙人的妻子。[21]甚至对于他的妻子妮娜，有时他的语气也足以让周围的人对他的妻子产生同情。她怎么能容忍被那样对待？而无论是对上还是对下——他都是同样直率。邦夏对待权势敢于直言不讳，在他给林登•约翰逊写的一封关于约翰逊总统图书馆一个展会的书信中写道："对我来说，在您的图书馆里唯一刺耳的音符就是政治运动展。主题很好，但是所做的展览没有任何一点设计感或是对于空间或墙的考虑...看起来完全像个差劲的贸易展销会。"约翰逊的回复是礼貌谦和的。[22]

邦夏是个慧眼识人才的伯乐。他可以把人们引进他的圈子，然后回馈他们。邦夏不在的时候，罗杰•雷德福从事委员会规划工作，他被一个伟大的人拉到一边："我要离开办公室去吃午饭，"他和我在一起，然后他说："你去哪里吃午饭？"我说："不知道。"他说："那让我们去这里吧。"之后，我们去了三明治店，并谈了些话..."[23]邦夏询问了他的背景、教育及建筑兴趣。"在我们谈论的内容中，"雷德福接着说："总是付出与索取，之后的几年一直是这样，你知道。"然而，他承认："有时不只是付出与索取，有时..."[24]其他人的感受也是这样：邦夏看到什么感兴趣的东西，一扇门就打开了。

在准备吉达国家商业银行的设计中，项目高级设计师汤姆•吉利安（SOM 1963–90）表示邦夏开始不喜欢他（"你是做三角设计的那位"）后来，邦夏看到了吉利安建议层叠"V"字设计，表示欣赏并拉他加入了这个项目。再后来，项目接近尾声的时候，吉利安的合作伙伴——建筑师弗兰索瓦•布洛克看到设计后提出：通风调节器的凹槽，看起来像装饰用的嵌线，设计在角落处不合适。邦夏同意了他的意见，并从落成的建筑中去掉了这些设计。然而，对于与他直接利益没关系的事情他也会出手参与。1971年，一个闹情绪的雇员琳达•弗兰纳里离开了SOM，写了一封长信给邦夏哀叹公司缺少设计支持，并批判新来的合伙人缺乏商业头脑。"邦夏先生，"她写道："您是唯一一个值得全公司人尊敬的合伙人。"她恳请他重振公司活力。"我确信您一定关心公司的未来，在您的严苛之下是对所有雇员的真正关心..."邦夏是否真的回复她的信，不得而知，但是信上有铅笔记录的电话号码。邦夏试图打电话给她——认为这封信值得保留[25]。他要告诉我们有关他本人的什么吗？或是邦夏想通过他的来信来说出一些他不能公开谈论同事的东西呢？

沉默的邦夏

邦夏工作的一个方面还有待考查。据说他曾非常近距离接触一批著名著名的艺术家和雕塑家？他与他们相处是否表现了不同的一面？当然，他不是个易于掌控的人。尽管所有的说法都是"团队方式"，当邦夏不满意伊萨穆•野口勇（Isamu Noguchi）的建议[26]时，还是要求娜塔莉重新设计康涅狄格通用人寿保险公司总部的东北场地。野口勇与邦夏的合作并不总是很愉快。"片面"野口勇用了这个词，"合作"意味着屈从于建筑师的意愿。尽管如此，他还用不同的语气描述了他与艺术家的关系。以他和让•杜布菲和亨利•摩尔的大量往来信件可以看出他的诙谐幽默，愉快的谈话，以及期待进一步会面的表述。具有代表性的是发给摩尔的这封附信（1972年7月31日），来自《纽约时报》关于戴维德•米钦森的"亨利•摩尔未发表的图纸（1972年）"的一篇评论。"希望你会喜欢该评论。似乎充满深思和感情，让人似乎很难把他和一贯闷闷不乐的约翰•卡纳迪先生联系在一起。"[27]与摩尔和杜布菲的往来邮件，尽管常常是处理业务的邮件但也非常愉快。在给杜布菲的信（1972年11月3日）中，他写道：大通银行前面设置他的"Group of Three Trees"后："你的到访让我异常开心，尽管我们多年来时常联系，如此近距离接触还是第一次。"以及给杜布菲的信（1972年11月22日），邦夏热情洋溢的写道："这给了我们无穷的温暖和亲密感。"[28]这只是客户与客户的关系吗？还是邦夏急于逢迎那些需要帮他完成建筑作品的人呢？也许可能...尽管他尽量不把自己称作收藏家，他对于艺术的投入似乎已经超出建筑方面的乐趣："我不喜欢'收藏家'这个词，它太过迷恋，而有些病态。首先你得先买一两样，然后你会买得越来越多，然后变成无论到哪里都无法停止的状态。"这也是邦夏将他的个人兴趣与公司谋合的一个方面。[29]他可能绝不会成为穿着粗花呢的乡村会所建筑师，但可能成为现代博物馆的托管人。艺术带给他接触进步商人的机会，也使他将自己的艺术爱好成为他公共形象的一部分。[30]邦夏享受甄选艺术品的过程，将它们放在大通银行的办公室里，与好友西摩•诺克斯二世（1898–1990）——美国水牛城海丰银行（Marine Midland Bank）主席，分享对于当代艺术的热爱。诺克斯向水牛城的奥尔布赖特美术馆（后来的奥尔布赖特-诺克斯美术馆）捐赠了大量（邦夏设计的）作品。

邦夏与他的艺术及朋友们的信件似乎表明他们都在将同一语言，也许从某种意义上来说，是这样的。邦夏相信他的建筑必须自己来说话。而从更大程度来说，正如他1972年在《纽约时报》的观点："我喜欢我的建筑自己来说话，起码代表我说话。"[31]在描述给奥尔布赖特的藏品时，他在1962年《水牛城新闻晚报》上说："让建筑自己说话。"[32] 在他与亚瑟•德雷克斯勒的长访谈中，莱

因霍尔德•马丁写道，他"几乎不承认建筑与分析性论述的交叉点。"[33] 十年后，他写信给欧文•勒德，婉拒了首届皇家建筑师协会韦斯本讲演邀请："我不喜欢向大规模团体讲话，四十年没这样做了。我同时相信我设计建筑应该代表我。"[34]而也许这是他和艺术家们分享的沉默？他的朋友计•杜布菲认为书面艺术必然不受欢迎：

"书面语言对我来说不是个好的方式。作为表达的工具，它似乎只传达了了无生趣的思维残迹，或多或少的像燃烧后的渣块。"[35] 事实上，亨利•摩尔对于发表雕塑作品意见有他自己的顾虑："对于雕塑家或画家在公共场合谈论或记录他们的工作，这常常是个错误。也许某些强烈欲望或压力的释放需要他对于工作的专注。"[36]艺术家不愿解释他们的艺术，或许可以解释邦夏自己对于不确定的沉默。也许这只有在SOM的环境下——拥有发言人和新闻发布、以及能干的项目经理们的大公司，才可能存在。

邦夏对公司惯常的漠视态度令很多才能遭忽视的合伙人（"欧文斯是一位非常优秀的销售员"）非常头疼。[37]他从未成功指导年轻设计师或将设计师技能提升到合伙人水平：办公室也只是为了便利而已，而他去了以后，他们还得管理。芝加哥办公室的发展得益于威廉•哈特曼管理成熟的格雷厄姆、纳什、戈德史密斯和卡恩的贡献。邦夏开始试图阻止查克-巴西特，他是在西海岸独立发展起来的，得到了欧文斯的支持。在华盛顿，欧文斯帮助戴维德-查尔斯的成长。如今，巴西特、纳什和查尔斯的"下一代"管理着SOM。邦夏到了迟暮之年似乎认同了SOM的团队理念。他在观看SOM五十周年纪录片时，发表了简短的发言回顾了他与SOM的早年经历，还批评影片只集中于六个人。"事实上，"他说："我们都是平凡人。如果我们只做自己，我们将一事无成。我们实际上是一个团队...不同程度地奉献自己，如果不能成为团队的一部分，我们就无法超越...我认为并没有很多人注定成为柯布西耶或密斯甚至是莱特。我认为我们在归功于大家方面做得不够。就这么多。"[38]

最后邦夏仍然保持着他的神秘，而我们可以更好地总结他对于SOM的贡献。尽管他贡献了很多优秀建筑作品，并不仅限于这些。不仅仅是他的做事风格，尽管人们首先关注到这方面。即使他不善于表达，邦夏还是相信在整个设计过程中起作用的重要方面：人性需求、抱负和

梦想。[39] 他同时认为建筑问题需及时解决，因为这里有经济和时间成本问题（因为他做事效率很高），他在尽可能达到最高艺术品质的同时平衡这一信念。最后，邦夏对艺术真正的热爱，他的艺术家信念，让人们确信这是他内核心品质中最有价值的部分。SOM不再会有第二个邦夏——时代在变化——而说服力、适应力、诚实和优秀仍是合作的根本。

1. 摘自戴维德·邦夏1945年9月18日写给他的儿子邦夏的一封信，关于与其未来儿媳一家会面。戈登·邦夏，建筑图纸及文件，埃维利建筑与艺术图书馆，图纸及档案部，哥伦比亚大学，通信，系列1:6（简称邦夏，建筑图纸及文件，埃维利图书馆）。

2. "他一旦打定主意就不放弃——成为建筑师、加入麻省理工大学、参加SOM小型实践、确认解决方案并坚持做下去，而并非不停地反思问题。"卡罗·克林斯基，SOM戈登·邦夏（剑桥，纽约，1988年），第332页。

3. 见例如詹姆斯·巴布1959年8月10日写给惠特尼·格里斯沃尔德关于善本图书馆的信，耶鲁大学档案，RU 22 YRG 2-A, 1963-A-002，141号箱，1285号文件夹。

4. 例如，见邦夏否认美国艺术学院成员资格的角色讨论，给罗伯斯·文丘里、戴维德·雅各布的信，"机构建筑师"《纽约时报》，1972年7月23日，20-21页。或关于阻止文丘里设计的华盛顿交通广场办公楼（1967年）。还可参考文森特·斯库里（Vincent Scully）文丘里（原出版于1989年），现代建筑及其它文章（普林斯顿，2003年），277-78页。

5. "来自贫民区的建筑师"财富57（1958年1月），第137-40; 210, 212, 215页。

6. 威廉·怀特（William H. Whyte）组织人（纽约，1956年），第7页。见"价值20亿美金的协会设计"，商业周刊，1954年12月4日，第96-102页。

7. "SOM建筑师，美国"（1950年秋），第5页。

8. "忙碌世界的设计师：职业心态"，新闻周刊（1959年5月4日），第97-100页语录。

9. 约翰·艾德里安和托马斯，"约翰与艾德里安和托马斯的谈话"，AA文件63（2011），第23页。

10. 罗杰·雷德福，罗杰·尼古拉斯·雷德福的口述历史，采访人：莎伦·赞恩（芝加哥：艺术学院，2008年），第141页。同时参考戴维德·雅各布"机构建筑师"第16页："这意味着（指二十世纪五十年代）他设计及管理了出自办公室的一切..."

11. 邦夏对于他管理的建筑非常明确，见克林斯基，戈登·邦夏，第335-38页。1962年以前邦夏影响的建筑初步列表：玻璃纤维大厦，纽约（1948年，已拆）；泛美生活，新奥尔良（1951年）；灌浆公园学校，斯克内克塔迪，纽约（1954年）；哈里康特学校，纽黑文，康涅狄格州（1955年）；史密斯学院宿舍（Cutter Ziskind楼），北安普顿，马萨诸塞（1956年）；CIBA/嘉基，阿兹利，纽约（1956年）；研究室，惠氏制药，拉德纳，宾夕法尼亚州（1957年）；福特基金会，纽约（1957年）；女童子军，纽约（1957年）；医疗大厦，休斯敦，得克萨斯州（1957年）；国际到达大厦，艾德威尔德/肯尼迪（1958年）；哥伦比亚广播公司实验和技术中心，康涅狄格州斯坦福德（1958年），通用磨坊食品公司总部，金色山谷，明尼苏达州（1958年）；教堂和冥想房，科尔盖特大学（1959年）；波

12. "邦夏是一部机器的关键齿轮，作为合伙人管理纽约大部分设计工作。其它办公室经常给他打电话咨询。""设计价值20亿美金..."1954年《商业周刊》，第103页（见注释6）。《财富》中写道："他的设计影响力有时候觉得离纽约办公室很远"1958年《财富》，第215页；（见注释5）。

13. "SOM区别的细节"1960年，《建筑论坛》，第124-29页，语录引自第124页。

14. Allan Temko，"美国建筑：外立面与框架"美国建筑师学会学报（1958年11月），第19-23页。

15. "仅供建筑师使用"，《建筑论坛100》（1954年4月），第172页。

16. 见1958年《财富》，第215页。

17. 1988年Krinsky，第138页（注释2）。

18. 见SOM档案（旧金山），工号137，箱号1722，"部门间沟通2"，约翰维斯1963年10月25日给威廉布朗的信，1963年11月1日给戈登邦夏的信；11月末约翰维斯给戴维德艾伦的信。

19. 见《梅芙斯莱文，戴维斯艾伦：在SOM从事室内设计的四十年》（纽约，1990年）J. A.，"SOM: The Chicago Office of Skidmore, Owings & Merrill," Interiors (January 1959), pp., 90-109。

20. J. A. "SOM: 芝加哥办公室"室内设计（1959年1月），第90-109页。

21. 对于像Frazar Wilde这样的客户，可能控制说服力。例如，在提供康涅狄格通用人寿保险公司总部规划过程中，罗杰·雷德福讲道："业主希望提供备选方案。我们做了六个方案，而只有一个是戈登先生感兴趣的。其它——你知道，会议将开始的时候，我们匆忙赶完其它五个，然后将集中做一个"罗杰·雷德福，《罗杰·尼古拉斯·雷德福的口述历史》，第44页。而在社交过程中，邦夏的说服力常常被人认为是粗鲁无礼。

22. 戈登·邦夏写给休斯顿·约翰逊总统的信，1971年6月1日，邦夏，建筑图纸和文件，埃维利图书馆，通信，系列1:4。

23. 《罗杰·尼古拉斯·雷德福的口述历史》，第35页。

24. 出处同上，第37页。

25. 邦夏，建筑图纸和文件，埃维利图书馆，通信，系列1:12。

26. 邦夏，建筑图纸和文件，埃维利图书馆，通信，系列1:4。

27. 邦夏，建筑图纸和文件，埃维利图书馆，通信，系列1:4。

28. 邦夏，建筑图纸和文件，埃维利图书馆，通信，系列1:9。

29. "邦夏和野口勇" 52，邦夏逐渐形成 Royal Barry Willis似的措辞："无私的市民服务是每个建筑师的责任"他在推荐加入当地艺术委员会的信中写道。Royal Barry Willis，建筑商业（纽约，1941年），第63页。

30. 他对贝蒂·布卢姆说："我想成为设计师和呆在那家公司的原因之一就是，在二十世纪三十年代早期，我觉得建筑是一个绅士的职业，他们都是俱乐部会员，他们都在俱乐部工作。以及很多类似的原因。那是我作为犹太人的思维方式——不是单纯为了工作"贝蒂·布卢姆采访邦夏的口述记录（芝加哥，1990年；2000年修订版），第230页。他给戴维德·雅各布的意见重复了上述内容。"机构建筑师"《纽约时报》，1972年7月23日，第16页。

31. 雅各布，"机构建筑师"第12页。

32. "让建筑自己说话"《水牛城新闻晚报》，1962年1月20日。

33. 见莱因霍尔德•马丁，"邦夏录音带：初步报告"。

《建筑教育学报54》（2000年11月），第81页。

34. 邦夏，建筑图纸及文件，埃维利图书馆，通信，系列1:5（无日期）。

35. "反文化定位"，杜布菲1951年12月20日在芝加哥艺术俱乐部的演讲，转载于《当代艺术的理论和文件：艺术家作品资料》克里斯汀•斯泰尔丝和彼得•霍华德•塞尔兹编辑（伯克利，2012年），第195页。

36. 引用于1937年《倾听者》的一篇文章，转载于1944年和1966年摩尔的著作。见《亨利•摩尔：作品与谈话》，艾伦•威尔金森编辑（伯克利，2002年），第20页。

37. 《戈登•邦夏的口述历史》，第49页。

38. 发给劳尔和简•穆斯的伯吉斯评论转述，1986年11月11日，邦夏，建筑图纸及文件，埃维利图书馆，通信，系列1:5。

39. 可参考例如，难以想象读到欧文斯关于下曼哈顿区改造为主题公园的琐碎描写，《居间空间：建筑师之旅》（波士顿，1973年），第164页。

Essayist Biographies

Nicholas Adams

Nicholas Adams is the Mary Conover Mellon professor in the history of architecture at Vassar College in Poughkeepsie, New York, where he has taught since 1989. He is a member of the editorial board of the Italian architectural magazine *Casabella* and author of *Skidmore, Owings & Merrill: SOM Since 1936* (2007). He has served as editor of the *Journal of the Society of Architectural Historians* and his essays and reviews have appeared in *Architectural Record, Harvard Design Magazine, and Arkitektur*, the Swedish review of architecture. He is currently writing a history of Gunnar Asplund's Law Court Extension in Göteborg. He has been a fellow of the American Academy in Rome and the Institute for Advanced Study, Princeton, and has also taught in the architectural schools at Harvard University, Columbia University, and UCLA.

Thomas de Monchaux

Thomas de Monchaux is an architect and writer. He teaches design at Columbia University's Graduate School of Architecture, Planning, and Preservation, and did his graduate work in Architecture at Princeton University. His architectural criticism and journalism has appeared in the *New York Times* and *The New Yorker* Culture Desk, in the journals *N+1*, *Perspecta*, and elsewhere. He received the inaugural Winterhouse Award for Design Writing and Criticism, and delivered the 2011 Myriam Bellazoug Memorial Lecture at the Yale School of Architecture entitled "Seven Architectural Embarrassments." A Contributing Editor at *Architect* magazine, de Monchaux is currently at work on *Dream House*, a book about cultural and personal histories of American houses and homes.

Kenneth Frampton

Kenneth Frampton was born in 1930 and trained as an architect at the Architectural Association School of Architecture, London. He has worked as an architect and as an architectural historian and critic, and is now Ware Professor of Architecture at the Graduate School of Architecture, Planning and Preservation, Columbia University, New York. He has taught at a number of leading institutions in the field, including the Royal College of Art in London, the ETH in Zurich, the Berlage Institute in Amsterdam, EPFL in Lausanne and the Accademia di Architettura in Mendrisio. Frampton is the author of *Modern Architecture and the Critical Present* (1980), *Studies in Tectonic Culture* (1995), *American Masterworks* (1995), *Le Corbusier* (2001), *Labour, Work & Architecture* (2005), and an updated fourth edition of *Modern Architecture: A Critical History* (2007).

John Harwood

John Harwood is Associate Professor of Modern and Contemporary Architectural History in the Department of Art at Oberlin College, Ohio. His research centers on the architectural articulation of science, technology, and corporate organization. He is an editor (beginning with issue 51) of *Grey Room*, a journal of art, architecture, media and politics published by MIT Press. His articles and reviews have appeared in *Grey Room, do.co.mo.mo, AA Files, Journal of the Society of Architectural Historians*, as well as in catalogs and edited volumes. His book *The Interface: IBM and the Transformation of Corporate Design, 1945–1976* was published in 2011.

Peter MacKeith

Peter MacKeith was recently appointed the Dean of the Fay Jones School of Architecture at the University of Arkansas. Previously he was Associate Professor of Architecture at the Sam Fox School of Design and Visual Arts, Washington University in St. Louis. He received his MArch from Yale University and his BA in Literature and International Relations from the University of Virginia. MacKeith directed the international Masters program in architecture at the Helsinki University of Technology, and previously taught design and architectural theory at Yale University and the University of Virginia. MacKeith has worked in practices in the United States and Finland and has written and lectured extensively in the United States, Finland, and across the Nordic countries on the work of Alvar Aalto, and on contemporary Finnish and Nordic architecture. He is the author of several books including *Archipelago, Essays of Architecture* (2006). He began work as editor of the *SOM Journal* in 2011.

Sarah Goldhagen

Sarah Goldhagen, the *New Republic*'s architecture critic, is a critic, theorist, and historian of the modern and contemporary built environment. The author of *Louis Kahn's Situated Modernism* (2001) and editor, with Réjean Legault, of *Anxious Modernisms: Experimentation in Postwar Architectural Culture* (2001), Goldhagen's writings have appeared in numerous scholarly and general interest publications, including the *New York Times, Architectural Record, The Chronicle of Higher Education*, and *Landscape Architecture*. Before deciding to devote herself full-time to writing, she taught for ten years at the Harvard Graduate School of Design. She is currently finishing a book on the experience of the built environment.

Sarah Whiting

Sarah Whiting is the Dean and William Ward Watkin Professor of Architecture at the Rice School of Architecture. Previously, she taught at Princeton University, Harvard's Graduate School of Design, the Illinois Institute of Technology, the University of Kentucky, and the University of Florida. As a teacher, writer, and designer, her work revolves around architecture's catalytic relationship to politics, economics, and society, focusing especially on the modern subject (individual as well as collective) and the way that this subject affects and is affected by architecture and the city. Whiting's writings on urban and architectural theory have been widely published in journals and anthologies. In addition to authoring the book, *Beyond Surface Appeal: Literalism, Sensibilities, and Constituencies in the Work of James Carpenter* (2010), she is a partner, with Ron Witte, of WW, an architecture firm in Houston, Texas.

Juror Biographies

Michelle Addington

Michelle Addington is the Hines Professor of Sustainable Architectural Design, Yale University. Prior to Yale, Ms. Addington taught at Harvard University, Temple University and Philadelphia University. Her background includes work at NASA/Goddard Space Flight Center, where she developed structural data for composite materials and designed components for unmanned spacecraft; she also worked as a process design and power plant engineer; and as a manufacturing supervisor at DuPont. She researches discrete systems and technology transfer, and she serves as an adviser on energy and sustainability for many organizations, including the Department of Energy and the AIA. Her chapters and articles on energy, environmental systems, lighting, and materials have appeared in many books and journals, and she recently coauthored Smart Materials and Technologies for the Architecture and Design Professions. She received a B.S.M.E. from Tulane University, a B.Arch. from Temple University, and an M.Des.S. and a D.Des. from Harvard University.

Stefan Behnisch

Stefan Behnisch studied philosophy and economics in Munich, then architecture at the Technical University of Karlsruhe. He worked as an architect in Behnisch & Partner before establishing his own practice, Behnisch Architekten, in 1989, together with his father Professor Günter Behnisch. In the following years, he founded additional branch offices of Behnisch Architekten in Los Angeles, Boston, and Munich. A rigorous advocate of sustainable design, his first building abroad, the Institute for Forestry and Nature Research in Wageningen, The Netherlands, became a milestone for innovative sustainable solutions. He has received numerous awards, most recently, in 2009 a Good Design Award in the category of "People," presented by the Chicago Athenaeum and the European Centre for Architecture Art Design and Urban Studies. Behnisch has held several teaching positions: the Eero Saarinen Chair Visiting Professor at Yale School of Architecture; the Miller Visiting Professor at the University of Pennsylvania, Philadelphia; the Harry W. Porter Jr. Visiting Professor at the University of Virginia School of Architecture; and is currently a visiting Professor at the École Polytechnique Fédérale in Lausanne (EPLF). He is a BDA, RIBA and AIA member, an NCARB certified architect, and an AIA Honorary Fellow.

Peter Rowe

Peter Rowe is the Raymond Garbe Professor of Architecture and Urban Design and University Distinguished Service Professor at the Graduate School of Design, Harvard University, and has taught at Harvard since 1985. Between 1992 and 2004 he served as Dean of the Faculty of Design, following appointments as Chairman of the Department of Urban Planning and Design, and Director of the Urban Design Programs. Previously, Professor Rowe was Director of the School of Architecture at Rice University and Vice President of Rice Center, an off-campus research institution in Houston, Texas. He recently served as Education Program Director of the Aga Khan Trust for Culture, and currently serves as Vice Chairman of the International Advisory Council of the Peoples Municipal Government of Wuhan, China, and is a member of the governing board of the UNESCO World Heritage Institute for Training and Research in the Asia and Pacific Region. He has also served as a board member of the Centre Canadien d'Architecture and the board of the Cities Programme of the London School of Economics. Professor Rowe graduated from Melbourne University, Australia, with a B.Arch (1969) and from Rice University with a MArch in Urban Design (1971). He also holds an AM (Hon) from Harvard University (1986).

Project Credits

Baietan: Heart of Guang-Fo Urban Design Master Plan
Guangzhou, China
Designed 2010

Client: Guangzhou City Planning Bureau, Guangzhou Land Development Center
Managing Partner: Gene Schnair
Design Partner: Craig Hartman
Consulting Partner: John Kriken
Design Director: Ellen Lou
Project Manager: Lucy Ling
Urban Design Project Team: Michael Powell, Naifei Sun, Keiko Nakagawa, John Sugrue, Noah Friedman, Luca Giaramidaro, Athina Loumou, Jin Zhao, Xuan Wang, Meehae Kwon, Hong Li, Tien-Yun Lee
Architecture Project Team: Mark Schwettmann, Aaron Jensen, Ross Findly, Kezhen Cao, Fernando Herrera, Alex Cruz
MEP Project Team: Roger Frechette, Arvinder Dang, Ruth Kurz, Arathi Gowda, Jose Rodriguez
Collaborators: Guangzhou Urban Planning & Design Studio, Guangzhou Transportation Planning Research Institute
Landscape Design: Hargreaves Associates
Transportation: CHS Consulting

Colpatria Calle 84
Bogotá, Colombia
Designed 2012

Client: Colpatria
Managing Partner: Jeffrey J. McCarthy
Design Director: Ross Wimer
Senior Designer: Jose Valeros
Project Manager: Heather K. Poell
Team Members: Andrés M. Montaña, Darya Minosyvants Stefanovic, My-Nga Lam, Rodrigo Buelvas
Structural Consultant: Bradley Young

Mechanical Consultant: Sergio Sadaba
Technical Coordinator: Lucas Tryggestad
Environmental Consultant: Sergio Sadaba
Sustainable Infrastructure: Sherwood Design Engineers
Real Estate Economics: CB Richard Ellis
Environmental and Habitat: ICF Jones & Stokes
Illustration: Christopher Grubbs
Rendering: Crystal CG
Rendering: Spine 3D
Physical Model: California Model and Design

New Los Angeles Federal Courthouse
Los Angeles, California
Designed 2012–13

Client: GSA (General Services Administration)
Managing Partner: Gene Schnair
Design Partner: Craig Hartman
Design Directors: Paul Danna, Jose Palacios
Managing Director: Michael Mann
Technical Director: Keith Boswell
Technical Designer: Steve Zimmerman
Project Architect: Susan Bartley
Interiors Leader: Naomi Asai
Team Members: Garth Ramsey, Josh Kenin, Julia Ovsenni, Jordon Gearhart, Tanya Paz, Sean Corriel, Marc Tanabe, Isshin Morimoto, Erin Kasimow, Amy Rangel, Winna Japardi, Qinghua Fan
Structural Consultant: Skidmore, Owings & Merrill: Mark Sarkisian, Eric Long, Andrew Krebs
Mechanical Engineer: Syska Hennessey Group
Electrical Engineer: Syska Hennessey Group
Plumbing Engineer: South Coast Engineering
Photography: Gerald Ratto Photography
Courts/Detention Planning: AECOM
Civil: PSOMAS
Landscape: Mia Lehrer & Associates
Blast: Applied Research Associates
Lighting: HLB Lighting

Acoustics: Newson Brown
Fire/Life Safety: Rolf Jensen & Associates
Vertical Transportation: Lerch Bates
Graphics: Skidmore, Owings & Merrill, Dyal & Partners
Food Service: Cini-Little
Cost Estimating Consultant: Clark Construction

The Strand, American Conservatory Theater (A.C.T.)
San Francisco, California
Designed 2012–14

Client: American Conservatory Theater
Managing Partner: Gene Schnair
Design Director: Michael Duncan
Senior Designer: Aaron Jensen
Project Manager: Gayle Tsern Strang
Technical Coordinator: Maurice Hamilton
Design Team Members: Eric Cole, Alex Cruz, Patricia Haight, Lisa Hedstrom, Jongsun Lee, Yuji Nishioka, Jessica Said
SOM Structural Engineering: Mark Sarkisian, Neville Mathias, Jeffrey Keileh
SOM Graphics: Lonny Israel, Brad Thomas, Nicholas Gerstner
Mechanical Engineering: WSP Flack + Kurtz
Theater Consultant: The Shalleck Collaborative, Inc.
Acoustics: Charles M. Salter Associates, Inc.
Historic Consultant: Page & Turnbull
Lighting Design: Pritchard/Peck Lighting
General Contractor: Plant Construction Company L.P.
Sustainability Consultant: Rick Unvarsky Consulting Services, Inc.

Image Credits

p. 28 © Gerald Ratto Photography Baietan model image
pp. 31, 32 © Crystal CG Baietan renderings
pp. 48, 49 © LAFC: ATCHAIN
p. 73 © image courtesy Ekain Jiménez Valencia
pp. 78, 80 © Eliasson images: Studio Olafur Eliasson
p. 118 The Yale School of Architecture grants permission for the reproduction of the article "Maison de Verre" from *Perspecta* 12 (1969)
pp. 120, 123 © Maison de verre Pierre Chareau: Photo Les Arts Décoratifs, Paris, Luc Boegly
pp. 118, 124, 125, 126 © Michael Carapetian
pp. 128, 129 © Kenneth Frampton

All other images courtesy of SOM unless otherwise noted. Every reasonable effort has been made to identify owners of copyright. Errors or omissions should be submitted to SOM and will be corrected in subsequent editions.

Acknowledgments

The Partners of SOM extend their thanks to Peter MacKeith, the Jurors, and to all those who have contributed to the represented work. We would also like to thank Robert Rubin, Carolina Windsor, Sergio Difilippi, Olin McKenzie, Joseph Kuhn, Bret Quagliara, and Colin Koop, in assembling, writing, and coordinating the materials for this *SOM Journal* 9.

Edited by: Peter MacKeith

Managing editor: Amy Gill

Copyediting: Eugenia Bell

Graphic design: SOM

Typesetting and reproductions: Weyhing digital, Ostfildern

Production: Ines Sutter, Hatje Cantz

Typeface: Arial MT

Paper: LuxoSatin, 150 g/m^2

Printing: Firmengruppe APPL, aprinta druck GmbH, Wemding

Binding: Conzella Verlagsbuchbinderei, Urban Meister GmbH, Aschheim-Dornach

Published by
Hatje Cantz Verlag
Zeppelinstrasse 32
73760 Ostfildern
Germany
Tel. +49 711 4405-200
Fax +49 711 4405-220
www.hatjecantz.com

A Ganske Publishing Group company

Hatje Cantz books are available internationally at selected bookstores. For more information about our distribution partners, please visit our website at www.hatjecantz.com.

ISBN 978-3-7757-3704-3

Printed in Germany